Sam T. Clover

Leaves From a Diary

A Tramp Around the World

Sam T. Clover

Leaves From a Diary
A Tramp Around the World

ISBN/EAN: 9783744717595

Printed in Europe, USA, Canada, Australia, Japan

Cover: Foto ©Andreas Hilbeck / pixelio.de

More available books at **www.hansebooks.com**

Leaves

From a Diary:

—A—

TRAMP AROUND THE WORLD

—BY—

SAM T. CLOVER.

---

*"With much good will the motion was embraced
To chat awhile on their adventures pass'd."*

CHICAGO.
M. D. KIMBALL, PUBLISHER,
170 MADISON STREET.
1884.

TO
MY FRIEND
FRANC B. WILKIE, ESQ.
THIS
LITTLE JOURNAL
IS
RESPECTFULLY
INSCRIBED.

LEAVES FROM A DIARY.

A TRAMP AROUND THE WORLD.

FIRST EXTRACT.

Fifteen hundred miles from home, a total stranger in a strange city, and with finances completely exhausted, is not an enviable situation to be in; but that was my position exactly, on a certain day in September some two or three years ago.

I had been in Denver about a week, having arrived there one dismal rainy day, after a long ride over the mountains and through the South Park, from the new mining camp at Gunnison City; the journey of three hundred miles having taken ten days to accomplish.

Leaving Chicago some three months previous for the far West, I had wandered aimlessly from camp to camp, through the mining district of Colorado, in search of a possible Eldorado, where I was to "strike it rich" and return home in glorious triumph, as, perhaps, I had presumptuously predicted. I forget the exact amount I *did* return with—but no matter.

Near Rico, in the San Juan Valley, I became acquainted with a party of miners, who were out prospecting; they were a jovial, reckless set of fellows, and with that free hospitality never to be met with elsewhere, cordially invited me to join them. My valise I had left at Silverton, but in the mountains one need not be particular, and my blue woolen shirt was eminently fitted for camping, especially where water was so plentiful.

For a week I stayed with my newly-made friends, and constituting myself cook to the outfit, proved to be of no small service, for of all things this duty is the most irksome to the true prospector.

It was a proud day for me when I could turn a "flapjack" by inserting a knife under the mass of half-cooked batter—that perhaps filled the entire bottom of the pan—and tossing it in mid-air, dextrously catch it on the blade and deposit the cake safely, without a splash, in the "skid" again.

The miners staked out several "claims" during my stay, and in one or two my name was entered on the notice with the rest. I even put in two hours' hard labor with pickaxe and shovel at assessment work on one claim, but having blistered both hands badly in the effort, concluded cooking was more my *forte*, so desisted. Perhaps that claim to day is worth millions of dollars, and I—one of the original owners—remain in total ignorance.

I was sorry to leave them; they were rough and wild, but were very kind to me at all times, and it was with deep regret that I parted company and returned to Silverton. From there I had my valise forwarded to Denver, after selecting a few necessary articles of clothing which I wrapped in my blanket, and slinging the latter on my back started out for a tramp across the San Juan Divide, *en route* for the

Gunnison country.

From Silverton to Animas Forks, thence to Mineral Point, Ouray and Los Pinos Agency, I pursued my way, arriving at the latter place on the third day. Several times during the tramp I was tempted to throw away my blanket, so irksome was the load, yet I hung to it through all the journey until I arrived at Denver, where I sold it to a second-hand dealer for a small sum.

At the Agency I met a young Chicagoan, a lieutenant of one of the cavalry companies, stationed about twenty miles below the post, on the Uncompaghre River. Learning where I hailed from, he invited me to visit the camp, and the ambulance wagon arriving that afternoon for mail we both returned in it.

I spent three days among the soldiers in the field, and it being just after the pay-master's visit, the boys were flush of money, and were eager to part with it. I saw more gambling in those three days than I ever expect to see again in as short a time. Officers and privates alike were possessed of the mania, and gave it full vent. One enterprising individual even had a roulette wheel running in full blast, and appeared to be doing a big business. I suppose that the poor devils get so sick of the monotonous inactivity of a long camp, with its unvarying round of duties, always the same day after day, that they become thoroughly demoralized, and being beyond the confines of all civilization, unconsciously verge upon a semi-barbarous state.

My new acquaintance was the senior lieutenant of his company, and, the captain being away on sick leave, he was in full command. The second day of my visit he received orders to take his company on a short scouting expedition to select a new site for a camp. This was gratifying news to him and the boys in blue, as it promised a change in the dreary blank of their existence, and it was not long before they were in readiness to the bugle-cry of "mount."

Loaning me a blouse and fatigue cap, my friend smuggled me into the party, I using his spare horse, and by keeping well in the centre of the company, I managed to escape the keen eye of the colonel—a regular martinet—who rode down from headquarters to see us off.

It was a glorious trip, and one that I cannot well forget. Towards evening one of the privates shot a magnificent elk, and that night around the campfire we dined luxuriantly on venison steak, broiled deliciously over red-hot coals. What stories those soldiers told, of course mostly relating to Indians and their modes of warfare—and how I did drink in, with ears wide open every word they uttered! The Meeker massacre was only a couple of months old, and one of the men had been with the first on the field, so that I heard the horrible story with all its revolting details. Poor Josephine Meeker! she is dead now but if what that soldier told be true it would have been better had she never been born.

Returning to camp next day, I took a reluctant farewell of the soldier boys, and taking advantage of the ambulance wagon's trip for mail, was conveyed back to the Agency in it. Again starting out on my pedestrian journey, I tramped boldly on toward my destination, passing through a Ute village on my way to the Cimarron, where I had the novel pleasure of witnessing a pony race, with Indian girls as riders.

I generally averaged twenty-five miles a day,

which was pretty good traveling in that section, where the alkali dust is nearly a foot thick, and the sun almost hot enough to cook eggs. I had some glorious meals on that route, one especially at Captain Kline's ranch on the Cimarron—composed of fresh brook trout, hot biscuits and roast venison—the remembrance of which, in latter days, when I was particularly unfortunate, haunted my dreams again and again.

My *entre* into Gunnison City was marked by a tragical occurrence. It was on Saturday afternoon when the dirty white tents and rough shingled shanties first met my view. The place was divided into "old" and "new" town. I put up at a hotel (?) in the former quarter, where I made close acquaintance with Gunnison water and its cleansing properties, aided by a bounteous use of good yellow soap.

In the evening I strolled over the newer portion of the town, or city, to speak correctly. The main and only street was chiefly lined with tents on each side, one or two rough pine shanties being the prominent exceptions. Such a motley crew of citizens I do not suppose could ever be met with but in such a frontier mining camp as this. Men of every nationality and description were here all worshipping at the same throne, and with a common ambition—gold!

It was like viewing an international fair to walk up and down the street and see the various articles spread out for sale along the walks, and hear the eternal din from a hundred different throats swelling out into one immense chorus and making night hideous. Men brushed by clad in true frontier style, red neckerchief and wide slouched hat, blue or gray woolen shirt, heavy mining boots, and round the waist a belt or scarf which was adorned with a revolver or bowie-knife conspicuously placed.

The sound of music (?) drew my attention to one of the largest and most pretentious-looking wooden buildings on the street. A dirty canvas sign stretched over the entrance, bore the device in flaring black letters, "Eureka Saloon," and it was evident from the crowd passing in and out it was liberally patronized. Following the tide I found myself in a regular " den " of the very worst description. A dance was in progress as I entered, the females—

some five or six in all—each trying to out-kick the other in a species of dance supposed to resemble the can-can. In the rear end of the room some twenty or thirty men were collected around a green table kept by one "French Pete," who was also the dealer. A murderous looking revolver was prominently resting at his right hand, and the "look-out" also sported its counterpart.

The game was "faro," and edging up to the table I found big stakes were being played for, one half-drunken miner having, when I arrived, nearly five hundred dollars on the board. He had been losing heavily, and was disposed to be "fighting mean;" what is known as "splits" had been dealt him three times in succession, on as many different bets, and with the last he half rose, and swore he was being "worsted."

This was too much for French Pete and his colleague to stand, and in a trice two revolvers covered the miner, whose hand also rested on a like weapon. Muttering an oath he loosened his hold and resumed his seat, but with the next turn from the box out came another "split." In a second three revolvers were whipped out, but the "look-out" shot first, and the miner fell.

In less time than I can tell, that saloon was vacated, and in company with about twenty others I found myself making lively time across lots to "old" town, where I quickly "turned in" at my hotel, for rest, entirely satisfied with my view of Gunnison by night. I heard afterward that when the city marshal put in an appearance all he found was the dead body of the miner on the floor, with the dress pockets turned inside out, and not an article of value to be found upon it. Whether any justice was meted out to the murderer, I cannot say, but at the time of my leaving I know nothing had been done.

Next day I had the good fortune to meet with a party of prospectors just about to start for Denver, after having been out since spring, prospecting. There were four in all, and they owned a good span of mules, a substantial looking covered wagon, with a complete camping outfit, including a portable cook stove. In addition to this, one of the party was possessed of a very good saddle-horse, whose acquaintance I made later on.

SECOND EXTRACT.

For a small consideration, I was allowed to join the party in their trip across the plains, promising at the same time to do an equal share of the work with the rest. It was slow traveling of course, the mules not being able to go faster than a walk, so that thirty miles a day was considered an excellent record. I was permitted to ride the spare horse nearly all the journey and often would speed ahead of the wagon some five or six miles, dismount and hobble the horse, then lie down in the cool shade along the Tumichi river and await the arrival of my comrades.

With the outfit was a good rifle and shot-gun and plenty of fishing tackle. The latter was in constant requisition, the mountain streams being abundantly stocked with fish, trout being especially plentiful. We shot a deer once during the mid-day halt and for two days feasted royally on the venison. Sage hens were also to be obtained very easily and barring a somewhat pungent odor the meat was really very appetizing.

My Rico apprenticeship served me in good stead on this trip, as none of the party could boast of their cooking powers—unless in making coffee—and many were the encomiums I received, on my skill with that choice morsel—the "flapjack." In crossing the South Park the heat from the sun was intense, so that we generally started very early, in order to make good time before Old Sol attained much power. Halting at noon for lunch and to rest and water the mules, we would all take a short siesta, then harness up—and plod on again until dusk when the final halt for the day was made.

It was my duty always to ride ahead and select our camping ground at night, as after leaving the Tumichi river water was much more scarce, and oftentimes we were compelled to ride on some distance beyond our usual day's quantum of miles in order to camp near a stream. We were generally very fortunate in this respect and once only suffered for want of water, the poor mules being the worse off

—we only being deprived of our usual luxury—coffee.

I enjoyed the trip very much, in spite of the monotony that the last three or four day's journey entailed, and was really quite sorry when the spires and chimneys of Denver were visible to the eye. I had made good friends of all in the party; we had been constantly together for ten days and I think I can safely say, were loth to part company, but of course our ways did not lie in the same direction and after a cordial handshaking we parted, they to seek their respective homes, I to take my own peculiar course.

It was here that I first determined to make the Grand Tour, and that, too, when my money was nearly gone. I had been in Denver three days when this brilliant idea was conceived, and during that time had been debating upon the policy of returning home to confess my error in ever leaving, and resume where I had broken off, or to continue my wanderings. Prudence whispered, "return;" but the desire for travel, seconded by a strong aversion to going back broke, carried the day, and from that time on I kept my face ever westward, until I finally halted at my starting point, having made a clean circuit of the world.

My personal outfit at this time was not elaborate but very serviceable, especially for the trip I contemplated. Having resolved to work my way round the world, I was of course prepared to rough it in many different ways, so my costume was peculiarly adapted to the position. It consisted of a stout pair of knee-boots, dark grey suit of clothes, blue woolen shirt and soft felt hat, all made to wear and warranted to last, which they did in spite of pretty rough usage.

It was not long before I met a kindred spirit whose aspirations, like mine, were fixed westward, and whose cash account was as easy to figure. California was the goal of his hopes, and over our last meal eaten in Denver we shook hands to make the "riffle" together. He proved to be a very cheerful companion, was decidedly Mark Tapleyish under difficulties, full of mother wit, and, having been over the road before, knew the ropes thoroughly. Our immediate destination was Cheyenne, W. T., distant from Denver about 140 miles. As we had no money, of course our only way to get there was to walk, and this we proposed to do. Perhaps the notes taken from my diary will better tell the story of my actual *debut* as a tramp:

Monday, 6th.—Started at 6 a. m. to walk to Cheyenne; my friend Charley had twenty cents, I thirty; lunched at Golden, 14 miles from Denver; walked steadily all afternoon; toward dusk left track to make short cut to next town, where we proposed halting for night. Lost our way, kept right along until near midnight, when, having sprained ankle, could scarcely lift my foot it was so painful. Finally crawled under some railroad ties piled up near the track, which a curve brought us to, and both being exhausted fell asleep.

Tuesday, 7th.—Found we had walked 35 miles; felt very tired; did too much first day. Breakfasted at Boulder on some bread and cheese which we obtained with our last dime. Good sleep in shade near Fair Grounds, after which had a refreshing swim. Walked to Longmont, having scored 25 miles. Went supperless to bed, the latter being an empty box-car on side track. Dreamed I was home reporting for Chicago paper at a banquet; saw all the good things spread out before me and was about to partake, when a kick on the shin from my restless comrade awakened me; turned over with a sigh and groan.

Wednesday, 8th.—Went up town, and at a bakery traded good silk handkerchief for couple loaves of bread, some cheese and half a pie; returned in triumph with my trophies, divided the spoils with Charley and another unfortunate who crawled out of next car; aided by cold spring water made capital meal. In spite of my swollen ankle, walked to Loveland, nearly 18 miles. Drew lots for supper, received "Hotel;" went to the kitchen (first appearance in this line) and in reply to modest request for food, was referred to woodpile. I left, but next day was glad to go back. Found car loaded with grain in bags; proved most luxuriant couch, and dropped peacefully to sleep.

Thursday, 9th.—Helped to clean engine on side track; driver gave me ride to Fort Collins. Went to restaurant, sawed wood for dinner and again for supper, having waited for companions to catch up. They concluded would wait at Ft. Collins for a day or two, and would meet me in Cheyenne, so in company with young cow-boy, started at 6 p. m. for Lone Tree. This was worst part of journey, as there is no water and no shade far nearly 30 miles, so determined to walk all night as being better than submitting to heat from blazing sun during day. Beguiled the first few hours by describing favorite dishes in the way of eatables we were most particularly fond of, and the justice each could mete out to this or that delicacy. Gradually became too tired to talk, settled down into dogged walk. Coyotes howled right and left, but none came near; watched the evening star mount higher and higher in the heavens, and wondered if morning would ever break again, or whether end of the world had come. With the rising sun we found ourselves close to deserted section-house about three miles from Lone Tree. Took off shoes and coat, made pillow and slept until sun was high above us. "Lone Tree" consisted of section house and a ranche. Drew lots and chose the former. Found little woman with big baby, wife of section boss, and who also boarded the laborers, doing all work alone. Carried several buckets of water for her, after which had first square meal since leaving Denver. Washed dishes, peeled potatoes and nursed baby. Little woman delighted; when husband returned offered me $15 a month and board, to stay; felt highly honored at offer, asked until next morning to consider; slept on kitchen floor.

Saturday, 11th.—Concluded not to stay, so not seeing my companion, set out for U. P. Junction, six miles from Cheyenne. At this place was horrified and shocked to find the dead body of the young cow-boy in freight room at Junction. Had stolen ride night before under freight train on "brakes," and fallen asleep; (presumably) his head was caught between running gear and floor of car; death, probably instantaneous?. He was buried at Cheyenne. Went to Camp Carlin, made friends with soldiers and was hospitably entertained. Found some had acquaintances with the cavalry on the Uncompahgre, so was made welcome on that account.

Next day I met my former chum Charley at the depot, he having arrived that morning. He had made good use of his time, having already discovered on a side-track some freight cars waiting to be made up with train for the West. Ogden was our next stopping-place and we both agreed that walking was not on the programme, so determined to steal a ride by forcible entrance into one of the cars loaded with perishable goods, as these are always forwarded without delay. To do this requires no little ingenuity, besides some risk, as, if caught by the yardmaster, it means a week in the lock-up; so we waited until dark before commencing operations. Charley had made the acquaintance of one of the fraternity (*i. e.* a tramp) bound in the opposite direction, who had agreed to help "spring" us in the car, as it is termed in tramp vocabulary. By the aid of a monkey-wrench we cautiously unscrewed the nuts that held the bolts of the sliding door in place, meanwhile keeping a sharp lookout for train men, who are naturally the sworn enemies of all tramps. The night was very dark, however, and we succeeded in forcing the door without detection, a flat board being used as a lever to hold the door open, while we crawled in. We were particularly fortunate in securing the aid of an accomplice, as it is very desirable to have the nuts replaced on the bolts after obtaining admittance to the car, as the train men make a special point of always inspecting the cars before starting, in order to see if they have been tampered with.

We had provided ourselves each with a bottle of water, and from the soldiers of the camp I had obtained a good supply of bread and meat, for we did not propose to starve on the way, as it takes from three to four days to make the trip. The water we carefully stored where the bottles would not break from any jolting of the car, and in a few minutes heard our friend replace the nuts and his low whistle told us everything was right. The hours that ensued until I fell asleep were not particularly pleasant ones—at least to me—for my companion was an old stager, and his low breathing soon told of his utter oblivion to the surroundings.

It was pitch dark in the car, and the air was heavy and stifling hot; my thoughts naturally took a despondent turn and played havoc with my imagination. I fancied we were about to become the victims of all sorts of railroad accidents, and pictured vividly the item we would make as served up by a western reporter upon the discovery of our mutilated corpses. Twice we were mangled and bruised beyond all recognition, and as many times were our charred remains discovered among the *debris* of the burned merchandise in the car. At last I fell asleep, thoroughly worn out, and when I awoke the car was in motion. The succeeding days and nights were almost a blank; the only knowledge we had of outside life was by hearing at intervals a noise overhead, occasioned by the brakeman tramping from car to car. We talked but little, ate and drank sparingly, and slept almost all the time. Two days and two nights of this was an experience I would never be tempted to repeat, and I was very thankful when the car was at last detached and sidetracked, from which we concluded we had arrived at Ogden.

We kept very quiet for some three or four hours, and then started a vigorous kicking on the door in order to attract attention, this being our only way to get out, as the yardmaster, hearing the noise, would naturally seek the cause. After repeated pounding we heard a voice crying out to let up, which we did. We were running no little risk in thus practically declaring ourselves tramps, as the law at Ogden gives all such one month imprisonment in the city jail, but it was our only chance to get out, and anything was preferrable to longer detention in the close atmosphere of the car. We did not propose to be caught without a struggle, so laid our plans accordingly. The seal being taken from the hasp of the door, the latter was slid back, and a voice commanded us to "Come out of that now!"

It was evidently quite early, very few men being in the yard, and from where I stood behind some boxes, I could see some distance up the track. Whispering to Charley, I told him to jump and run, and at a signal we leaped together, and escaping the clutches of the yardmaster, who proved to be rather aged, we lit out as fast as our cramped limbs would carry us. For the first few minutes I ran blindly, being almost dazed by the sudden transition from the darkness of our prison to the broad light of day. But the pupils of the eye gradually got accustomed to the change, and, pausing for breath, I found we were safe from pursuit.

THIRD EXTRACT.

Upon inquiry we found that we had stumbled upon the Salt Lake branch road, so thanking our lucky stars, we kept steadily onward, hoping to reach the Mormon City before night. Here I was fortunate enough to fall in with an old Chicago friend, who treated us like princes during our short stay in that beautiful valley. But Utah was not California, and we were anxious to be moving, so on the third day I said good-by to my hospitable friend, and with my comrade started back to Ogden. We arrived just as an emigrant train was about to pull out, and, jumping aboard, I went to the conductor and told him our fix. He agreed to carry us to the end of his division, after a little parley, giving us to understand it was because we had not attempted to steal a ride that made him so lenient. At the end of this section a kind-hearted brakeman took us in charge, and we rode to the end of his division in the tool chest attached to the caboose, it being under his immediate supervision. The next ride we made was between the tender and mail car of a through express, which carried us to Reno, Nevada, before the conductor discovered our presence. Then, for the first time, we did a little "drilling," *i. e.*, walking, but, before night, at a small station, managed to bribe a brakeman on a freight train, with a pocket-knife and pair of suspenders, in consideration of which we were allowed to hang on to an iron ladder, between two cars, all night long. By carefully watching the conductor's movements, we managed to stick to that freight until it reached Sacramento, Cal. Here Charley felt at home, and it being well toward evening, led the way to one of the river wharves. We found a boat almost ready to steam out for 'Frisco and by skillfully dodging the gate keeper managed to steal aboard unperceived, when we at once stowed away among a pile of freight on the lower deck forward. A calm sense of rest stole over me as I lay there, snugly hid, and gazed up at the shining moon, shedding her benignant rays upon the surface of the water, as we glided swiftly down the Sacramento river. The last I remember was kicking Charley for snoring so loudly, being afraid he would arouse the deck hands, and then I was in the land of dreams. When I awoke, we were moored to the wharf at San Francisco and the freight was being rapidly unloaded; our long and hard-fought trip was over, at least for the present, the Golden Gate lay right ahead and the city of hills and red-wood dwellings was open to our critical investigation.

Breakfast was naturally our first thought, the second, how to obtain it; neither of us had a cent, nor had we anything available to raise money upon; all desirable articles we possessed at the start, having long since been parted with to help soften the hearts of the various brakesmen we happened across while on the tramp, and into whose good graces we had been anxious to ingratiate ourselves.

My comrade, however, was not long in solving this conundrum, and confidently led the way up Market street toward the business center of the city. Our road led past the magnificent Palace Hotel, with its hundreds of windows about which I had read not a little. but the hasty glance I gave it did not impress me very deeply as to its pre-eminence, so far as architecture went, over some others I had seen, and I thought of our State Street hostelrie, away back at home, and heartily wished I were inside it. A small, and very dingy-looking store on Dupont Street closely verging on the Chinese quarters, was where my companion finally halted and into which he at once entered. Fifteen minutes later he emerged, and in answer to my look of inquiry, carelessly jingled some silver pieces in his pocket; it was very evident his mission had been successful and we lost no time in getting outside of the first square meal it had been our good fortune to sit down to for weeks. Our hunger appeased, we began to review our position. Charley's destination was Los Angelos, where his folks resided, and as he had been absent from them two years, he was naturally anxious to get home, and exhausted his best arguments in the vain effort to induce me to accompany him thither. I had other plans, however, and was not to be dissuaded from them, so, seeing I was determined as to my course, he finally gave in, and after generously dividing his stock of borrowed capital we parted.

The next three or four hours I spent in wandering aimlessly about the principal streets of the city and in feasting my eyes upon those prominent places of interest, more or less familiar to me from descriptive accounts gathered from time to time in newspaper articles. About three in the afternoon, as I stood in contemplative mood on the steps of the Post Office building, cogitating as to my next move, I was accosted by a rather dapper-looking, sharp-eyed man who inquired if I were not from Cincinnati. I quickly undeceived him on this point and in the conversation that ensued casually made known my situation, thinking perhaps he might be able to assist me in the furtherance of my scheme, which was to ship before the mast on any of the foreign-bound vessels then lying in port. Vessel business, however, was not in his line as I soon discovered. Finding I had not dined he took me to dinner, and during the progress of the meal unfolded a little plan of his own to which he required an assistant. The State fair was about to be held at Sacramento and he wanted me to go with him there and "tend" a stand in a large booth, where I was to preside over the sale of some precious "eye-water," my new acquaintance giving me to understand that he was a "doctor" and the inventor and sole agent on the Pacific coast for the "most inestimable liquid treasure for weak eyes ever yet discovered." He was a beautiful, smooth talker, this "Dr." Queechy, and I imagine there were few moves on the world's board that he was not fully posted on. While I felt confident he was a "quack" and his "medicine" trash, I thought there could be no harm in accepting his proposition for a few days, especially as he offered me a good percentage on all the "eye-water" lotion I should sell besides paying my food and lodging while the fair lasted; so I accepted his terms and agreed to go at once to Sacramento, as the fair opened next day.

We had big flaring cards posted around the stand setting forth in large type the virtues of the wonderful and miraculous "eye-water," compounded by that prince of philanthropists Dr. Queechy; also, on the stand were distributed a number of small dodgers, purporting to be testimonials from distinguished patients from all parts of the Union who had used the celebrated lotion with the most beneficial results.

Here I staid all day, giving out hand-bills to the country visitors as they strolled past, and selling them my "eye-water" at fifty cents per bottle, (with full directions for use accompanying each purchase.) I took in fifteen dollars the first day, and after locking up the stock in a large box, retired in high glee to a cheap hotel where I enjoyed the luxuries of a good square meal and a bed. Meanwhile I had seen nothing of my employer, but as he had informed me he should be very busy I supposed he would be visible next day.

In the morning, I repaired to the stand and fixed the stock ready for business. What easy victims those Californians were to the "doctor's" charms; I know now that the famous "eye-water was nothing but *aqua pura*, with (as the "doctor" tersely put it) the taste taken out; but how it sold,! That day I took in nearly twenty dollars and still the professor had not shown up, not that I cared very much but I thought his non-appearance strange.

The fair lasted four days and at the close I was

possessed of nearly ninety-five dollars in gold and silver; bottles all gone and my patron still *non est.* Chancing across a policeman, with whom I was on speaking terms, I described my employer and inquired if he knew him. He did. I then learned for the first time why I was employed and the cause of his disappearance. The "eye-water" business was a "blind," and the pseudo doctor's real profession was that of a gambler. He was a faker, or professional swindler, and in conjunction with an accomplice, had hired a carriage and team, bribed all the policemen on the grounds to wink at his business, and had introduced his latest effort—a lottery scheme, on an entirely new system. By the payment of a dollar the victim received a check on which was printed a number supposed to be equivalent to a prize. He was a cunning operator, as his *modus operandi*, explained by my friend, the policeman, will show. The purchaser pays a dollar and in return gets ticket No. 40. The gentlemanly agent offers him five, ten or fifteen dollars for it. He refuses, thinking it a fifty-dollar prize or perhaps larger. "Wont take fifteen for it, eh?" says the dealer. The answer is in the negative.

Round goes the wheel, No. 40 draws a blank. On the contrary, if he accepts three or four dollars for the ticket, he finds that it has drawn twenty, thirty or fifty dollars, as the case may be. This then was his real business, and as the policeman remarked "he drove a slashing trade." But the first day's transactions settled him; he wanted too much. In the evening a burly Californian, one of the victims, discovered the imposition, and quietly gathering a few friends sought out the clever swindlers. They smashed the lottery arrangement into splinters, which, by the way was quite a work of art, and then gave the couple five minutes start. They needed no second hint to leave town for they saw the gentlemen of the "glorious climate of California" meant business, and they hastily cleared for parts unknown. This of course, explained his not appearing to receive the dividend for the sale of the "eye-water," and I remained sole legatee, provided he did not appear to put in a claim later.

FOURTH EXTRACT.

Returning to 'Frisco, I replenished my somewhat dilapidated wardrobe and purchased a small valise; then began making inquiries around the wharfs for a berth in any of the ships lying in the bay. Despite all efforts I found it impossible to ship in any capacity, and I made up my mind that "running away to sea" was not quite such a fairy tale as the story books always led me to believe. I wanted to see Australia, that being the farthest point I could think of, so not being able to work my way I concluded to pay the passage money provided I had enough. It went against the grain though to do this, for a regular thorough bred tramp would rather work or beat his way (especially the latter,) anywhere rather than pay, no matter if he had ten times the fare, and although I was a new hand, the principles, I regret to say, were at that period inculcated in me.

Not being able to ship, and finding it equally hard to stow away, I repaired to the office of the S. S. Company for information as to passage money, dates of sailing, etc. This is what I read: First class to Australian ports, $200; steerage, $100. To Sandwich Islands, first-class, $75; steerage, $30. I had a little over $75 left, and a boat was to sail that same afternoon for Sydney, at two o'clock; it was then eleven. What did I do? I argued Sandwich Islands was just as good as Australia to me, and if I had to *pay* I would get the best, so without any more self-questioning on the subject, I stepped to the desk, put down four twenty dollar gold pieces and my name was entered on No. 38, upper berth, for Honolulu.

I had not much baggage to carry aboard; a few necessities in the way of linen were stored away in my valise, together with one or two books, that was all, and of farewells I had none to take. At five o'clock I was passing through the Golden Gate *en route* for the Sandwich Islands, the Pacific coast was fast disappearing from view, and the music of the waters lapping against the ship's side soon lulled me into forgetfulness, and I went to sleep and dreamed I married a rich planter's daughter and was crowned king of the Cannibal Islands.

The somewhat short voyage was accomplished without any particular incident worthy of note. Of course I was horribly sea-sick at first, but I soon recovered, and during the balance of the trip enjoyed myself hugely. The first night on shore at Honolulu was disappointing; I had imagined the place to be a tropical elysium overflowing with delicious fruits and beautiful flowery groves, where the soft balmy air would lull one into forgetfulness of all the harsh outer world; but the actual realization was a shock that I did not easily recover from.

Mosquitos by hundreds and thousands, attacked me as I vainly tried to woo sleep to my senses, and I suffered tortures until morning, when I managed to crawl into my clothes, weak from the loss of blood.

I had the pleasure of seeing his majesty King Kalakaua during my short stay. It was not the first time either; some five years previous, during his tour of the States, he had visited Chicago, and on its Board of Trade made a little speech, in my hearing. He did not appear greatly changed; I saw a stout well-built man, rather tall and of a dusky bronzed hue; very dark side-whiskers and moustache adorning a somewhat sensuous face. Dressed in a genteel suit of black, with a tall silk hat, he reminded me very much of a colored representative in Congress; or better yet, coachman to a wealthy private banker.

He is the people's choice for ruler, but is by no means the legitimate heir to the throne, Queen Emma—not his wife, however—a dignified, intellectual looking woman of perhaps thirty-five or forty, enjoying that distinction. I had an excellent opportunity of viewing her majesty's face on one occasion, and was much impressed by her natural dignity of bearing and intelligent countenance, which asserted itself in spite of her dusky color.

The day after my arrival, while strolling around the town, I came upon a number of the native Kanakas who had assembled in front of the post-office building and were waiting for the distribution of the mail brought by the steamer the night previous. As this takes place only once a month it is quite an event and is eagerly looked for. There was much jostling, laughing and loud talking among the natives, but it was a good-natured crowd, and all seemed happy and devoid of care. Presently a window was thrown open, a face appeared, a name was called and in response a tall young native stepped to the aperture, and as the mail was thrown to him, called out in his native tongue, with a stentorian voice, the superscription on each letter. Did the person happen to be on the farthest edge of the crowd, the letter or packet was passed over from hand to hand until it reached the owner. Were the fortunate recipient a young girl, as not infrequently happened. many a good natured joke and laugh were passed at her expense, while the letter was *in transitu*, and while of course I could not understand what was said it was easy to guess the purport.

I was not a little surprised at first to see these Islanders receive so many letters. The schools planted by the missionaries have done good work, however, and the young natives, absent from home on a cruise, take every opportunity to write to their friends at home. A great many of the male Kanakas ship on whalers, they being especially adapted to this class of sailoring, and make excellent boatmen on a long pull for a "spermer."

It was from this place I made my *debut* as a sailor before the mast. My finances being exhausted, and not possessing the means of replenishing—no work being obtainable, I boldly offered my services to the mate of a steamer, then lying at the wharf. Two of his men having levanted from the ship— which had been detained on account of repairs needed in the machinery—he was left short-handed, so, after a little parley, consented to ship me, and I signed articles for Sydney.

I was assigned to the port watch, and was expected to turn to with the regular crew, go aloft when required, scrub paint, wash decks, handle cargo, and, in fact, do all that was expected of an ordinary seaman. I was philosopher enough, however, to adapt myself to circumstances, and never grumbled at the work, and it certainly *was* hard. On the way from San Francisco I had beguiled the time by reading, and Dana's "Two Years Before the Mast" was a favorite book to me at that period. In it I remembered the one and only commandment in use on his ship, and I fully appreciated the force of it later. It was: "Six days shalt thou labor, and do all thou art able, and on the seventh holystone the main deck and scrape the cable."

I shall never forget the first time I went aloft. It was night, and we were two days out from Honolulu. The wind was blowing very fresh from dead ahead, and the watch was ordered up to make all snug aloft. It had just struck two bells—one o'clock morning—was very dark, and all I could make out was a dim shadowy mass above. I really had no desire to have any closer acquaintance either, so quietly stowed myself away behind a mass of coiled rope hanging to a belaying pin. But the second mate, who was in charge—a regular bull-dog—had spotted me, and with an oath ordered me aloft. I looked at him, glanced up at the uncertain clouds above, and concluded to go, being politely urged to quicker travel by a threatened visit from heavy sea boots. I did not render much assistance that time in furling sail, but stood clinging to the main-mast at the main-yard, shaking all over, and not at all reasured by my comrades' kind injunction to " Hang on with your eyebrows, Johnny!"

But after that first experience, I enjoyed the delightful sensation of climbing aloft, and there to drink in the glorious prospect. Being light and active, my post was at the extreme end of the yard at the main-top-gallant-sail. Here, resting on the foot-rope, and grasping the running gear, I would many a time stand and gaze down upon the ship's deck, which resembled a snake, in its narrow proportions, cutting through the water, and the wonder was how the vessel could possibly preserve its equilibrium.

When off-watch and in my bunk, below in the fo'castle, I would lie and listen to the sailors spinning yarns, the swish of the waves upon the ship's side, and gazing at the eternal green hue presented from the dead-light at my berth, finally drop off to sleep.

Handling cargo on a sweltering hot day, down in the ship's hold, where the thermometer stands anywhere from 90° to 110°, is the hardest part of the duties that an ordinary seaman is subjected to on a passenger steamer, and I found it so to my cost. To spend six hours there under direct supervision of an unfeeling mate, who has nothing but curses to bestow for the slightest mishap, is no child's play, but I managed to grit it through, always consoling myself with the thought that later I should be alive to laugh over my bitter experiences.

I stood it bravely for three weeks, but when we arrived at Auckland, New Zealand, I concluded I had had enough sailorizing for a while, so in turn, I took French leave and bade the ship adieu.

As a city, Auckland, to an American, presents some peculiar features. Walking down the main street, after six o'clock, any evening in the week, except Saturday, he would be astonished at the prison-like solemnity of the place. Nearly every store-front is strongly guarded with large wooden shutters, firmly secured by a heavy iron bar, running transversely the whole length of the windows, which gives the street an air of desolation and blankness utterly indescribable.

Excepting in the bar-rooms—or, by courtesy, "hotels"—not a light is to be seen; no handsome goods displayed; no gas-jets burning brightly in the windows; nothing but a dreary, wooden blank. After San Francisco, with its many calcium lights and handsome show windows, open upon every street, it is like going from the rush of busy Broadway to a country graveyard.

FIFTH EXTRACT.

It was a new experience to me to spend Christmas and New Year's without the usual concomitants —snow and ice—and I must confess I prefer our winter festival to the tropical one; it seems more real, and then, in the latter all one's dear old legends and memories are at a discount. No fire burning, no merry sleigh-bells, no steaming pudding, no turkey with its rich, crimson sauce; all these are conspicuous by their absence. One may get plenty to eat, but the appetite that comes with the healthy, cold Christmas is sadly wanting. The Arctic regions even would be preferable to celebrate in to this warm climate.

I did not stay long at Auckland; in spite of repeated efforts to obtain employment I was unsuccessful, so I again migrated, and Wellington, the city of eternal storms, was where I brought up. The wind blows here a fearful hurricane continually, and it is a standing joke for dwellers in neighboring cities to affirm that no matter where a Wellington man may be visiting, as he turns the corner of a street he involuntarily grasps his hat in order to steal a march on old Boreas.

In this town my affairs grew somewhat desperate. The German "Wander Year" may be all very well for the young native in his own country, but if he ever met with such a clannish lot of people outside the pale of home, as did I, methinks he would not succeed very well. When I applied for work the accent betrayed my nationality, and I was informed repeatedly, as was perhaps natural enough, only I could not think so, there were plenty of colonials who wanted work, and to them would be given the preference. However, my philosophy never allowed me to despair, and I remember when I had eaten nothing for forty hours, walking along the streets with my belt tightly buckled up, engaged in composing humorous rhymes to accord with my woe-begone condition. I will not inflict them on the chance reader, though, but they served at least to distract my thoughts.

In this extremity I applied for a position in an American circus that was showing through the colonies, and being willing to work was hired as a canvas man. I had previously considered sailor life hard work, but it was not a patch to that of canvas man to a circus. Driving stakes for the large tent at the show ground was the toughest of all, and but for hunger I certainly should have backed out.

The men are divided into squads of six, each man being armed with a heavy sledge hammer, with which to drive stakes. Standing in a circle round the billet, the first man would tap the pin into an upright position, followed by a blow from his next neighbor, then each man would strike in turn until the stake was down far enough; this operation being repeated until the entire circuit of the tents had been made. The perspiration would pour down in streams, and the arms ache fearfully, but one did not dare stop to rest or the balance would be thrown out. I was very glad when they transferred me to the property man, and for the few succeeding weeks, while with him, the only name I answered to was that of " Props." My duties in this line were numerous and varied. On arriving at a "show town" the first thing to be done after the ground had been staked out, was to put up the dressing-room tent, transfer the properties from the cars to the grounds, and range the performers' trunks in their respective places around the dressing-room. By this time the "boss" canvass man, with his force, would have the big tent up, and we, the property boys, were ready to place in position the many contrivances used during the performance, such as leaping boards, parallel bars, swinging poles, bicycle wire, trapezes, and a hundred other ingenious devices peculiar to a circus. The heavy work being done, "Old Props," as the performers designate the "boss property man," allotted us individual tasks, which generally occupied our time until the afternoon performance began. My chief duty was to make the thin, tissue paper balloon hoops, used by the riders and clowns, when in the ring; from thirty to fifty were used every day, and I found it a back-aching, and decidedly temper-trying job, especially at Wellington, where the wind, sweeping in under the walls of the tent, blew my balloon, against the corners of trunks, bursting them as fast as made, and scattered my stock of tissue paper in every direction.

A property boy is the recognized butt of every employe belonging to the circus, and, as a general thing, he receives enough kicks and curses to kill any ordinary mortal. Talking back is out of the question. I once heard of a new boy who attempted to refute an accusation hurled at him by the ring-master on some groundless charge, and he suddenly disappeared. The boys said his ghost used to haunt the ring—he was "ring boy"—and stalk behind the clown during the performance, until one day the manager died from the effects of a prolonged spree, when the spirit ceased its visitations.

If the tumbler missed his leap, something was wrong with the running board, and "props" as a body was eternally damned in a shower of invectives. Did the rider do a bad act, "props" was to blame for the uneven ring or faulty "pad;" no matter if he was in no way connected with fixing the trappings of the horse; *somebody* must be censured, and custom had marked "props" for the victim. The lady riders were equally liberal in their cavilings, and the poor devils often wished they were dead—I know I did. And yet they were kind in their way, and did not mean to be harsh. They were only acting as habit had accustomed them to. Every actor, at least a circus performer, is a chronic grumbler, and it is characteristic of them to shirk all responsibility to the shoulders of poor "props," right or wrong, and so he must swallow it all and with it his self-respect. It was a bitter thing to do at first, but gradually I grew hardened as I observed the matter-of-course air with which "old props" received all the insinuating remarks, and like many other "experiences," I put it down as a lesson to be strictly memorized and stored for future use; perhaps after all, the discipline did me no harm.

Life behind the scenes in a circus troupe is not of a particularly edifying nature. To begin with, a canvas man is necessarily of the roughest and toughest of his sex. A drunken, thieving lot of men, homeless, friendless and utterly destitute of all self respect. I have seen men come in at night after the show, perhaps a little the worse for whisky, and taking off shoes and coat arrange them as a pillow, using spare canvas for a covering, and in the morning they would be unable to find hat, coat, shoes, and oftentimes their hard earnings all gone, having been relieved during the night by their comrades. Worse than common thieves, they prey upon each other and *honor* is a quantum totally unknown to their creed.

The performers, to advance a grade, are as a rule very uneducated except in circus ways, and books they seldom touch, although great on sporting papers. The ignorance of the "talented and charming young bareback rider," a girl of seventeen, was really deplorable. Her mother, also a rider, had introduced the little one in the dressing room directly after a beautiful "act," at a matinee performance, amid the yelling of the clown, the roars of the lions in the menagerie adjacent, and the rough jokes of the male performers on the other side of the canvas partition. Born on a bed hastily snatched from the property wardrobe, and composed of a heterogeneous mass of elephant trappings, old tights, spangled suits and camel coverings, she had lived in the same atmosphere ever since. Her father she never knew, and at the age of six her mother was thrown from the horse she was riding and broke her neck, leaving the little daughter alone and at the mercy of her associates. But to their credit, be it said, they did their part well—as they best knew how—and she was formally adopted as the "daughter of the circus." All took a hand in her education, and while her grammar and geographical knowledge were, perhaps, neglected, her professional studies were pursued with earnestness and avidity, so that when still quite young she gave great promise of a brilliant future in the "realms of the ring." Although fully up to the latest slang of the day, I found her to be of a decidedly innocent turn of mind; totally ignorant of the world outside the circus; fond of gay dresses and "bravas" from the admiring audience, yet beyond that devoid of a single ambition.

While I was with the circus she had no less than eight proposals for her hand, from the troupe, among whom were a number of new performers; but love was something decidedly foreign to her nature, and she treated each new suitor in the same way; laughed in their faces, referred them to the ring master and went on feeding the monkeys or practicing a new jig step in the side show, as it happened. On one occasion, when leading her horse around the ring, while the clown was working the risibilities of the audience, I overheard a most impassioned proposal from one of the balloon holders, who was in the ring, and near whom we halted just as the clown had reached the climax of his joke. It was delivered during the yelling of the delighted crowd, and he really made a fervid appeal, but her only answer was a laugh as she whipped up the horse with a "Hi! Ya!" and in less than a minute was jumping head first, not into his arms, but into the balloon he held in his outstretched hand.

This young fellow, by the way, was an exception to the ordinary run of circus performers. He was considered the best leaper, the best rider, and was accounted the best looking man in the troupe, and I am certain he was the best educated. His parents were said to be quite wealthy, and he had graduated from Harvard, but his bohemian instincts got the ascendency, and his gymnastic course of training was an open sesame to the ring, after a year or two of hard practice. His specialty was riding four horses bare-back, but in spite of this, when waiting for his "act," he was obliged to doff a "spike-tail" and make himself useful with the fellows in the ring, as the manager allowed no loafing. He took his dismissal with a great deal of composure, however, and next day told me, was revenged by seeing the clown receive the mitten, even that individual being tempted to try his fate. There seemed to be an epidemic existing among the unmarried performers, they nearly all caught the fever. I suppose it was caused by the tropical weather. Sensible girl; last time I heard of her she was unmarried, and I saw by an eastern paper she was engaged in sending her monthly savings in postal remittances to the New York Post office.

Like the rest of the professional gentlemen, the circus performer is very improvident. Generally, he runs to diamonds, when flush, and is very partial to champagne and other fluids that come high, not worth drinking otherwise; add to this, fondness for the opposite sex, and the solution is easy. Wine, women and diamonds: a strong enough trio to undermine any man. There was one smart fellow who travelled with the circus—"candy-butcher,"—I believe he was, who made a practice of loaning money to the performers on their diamonds; as he was an excellent judge of a stone, he was seldom taken in, and he once informed me privately, that he considered it a mighty poor season when he did not clear two thousand dollars. Once pawned, the actor finds it hard work to redeem the article, and the result is the loan broker often clears from 70 to 80 per cent on his investment.

For three weeks I filled the honorable (?) and arduous position of "props" to the greatest set of grumblers on the road, but at the end of that time an incident occurred which occasioned a decided change in my mode of living, and of which I was not slow to take advantage.

SIXTH EXTRACT.

Among the many startling and world-renowned wonders the show advertised was the "daring bicycle act, performed in mid-air, on a wire cable stretched from pole to centre-pole, at a height of sixty feet from the ground." The bicycle was fitted with a double trapeze which hung suspended below the wire cable and was attached to each side of the machine, the latter running in a deep groove over the wire. While the rider worked the treadles above and ran the bicycle from pole to pole, forward and backward, three gymnasts performed some very clever evolutions below and held the audience spell-bound as they gazed at the startling exhibition.

Soon after leaving Wellington, the rider of the bicycle was taken sick, so that he was unable to perform his share of the "great sensational act." As this was one of the leading features of the show, and had been extensively filled, it was absolutely neccessary to get a substitute to fill his place. One would imagine this would be easy enough among thirty or forty performers composed of gymnasts, acrobats and riders, but such was not the case. All these individuals had a specialty of their own, and in their line were very clever and daring; but come to try them on a new tack they soon sheered off. "You cannot teach an old dog new tricks" is a very true saying. I have observed the force of it many a time. These actors were bred to do certain things on a certain level; raise them above a given altitude, and they failed at once, as it proved. On the horizontal bars, none were more skillful or daring than those we had; you could find few better leapers or tumblers anywhere, or finer horsemen than those attached to the circus; but all their acts were done on a level; they had been accustomed to it for years, and it meant nothing extraordinary to them, although the acme of daring perfection to an outsider.

Each individual in turn mounted to where the bicycle swung on the wire, gave a look below—usually one glance was enough—came down, and at once declined the proffered position. Their answers varied but little—it was "too high, thank you; get some one else; this is not what I hired out for." The manager was in despair; some one must be sacrificed, or the act would have to be "cut" and the public would be furious.

Finally, he was informed that the new "props" had been a "sailor" and perhaps would undertake the billet. At this time I was reckless enough to attempt anything, no matter how foolhardy or dangerous it might prove; and upon being interviewed by the manager announced my willingness to try it. Accordingly, that very morning, after ring practice with the horses, I mounted to the wire, and after the trapeze-performers had taken their respective positions below to steady the machine, I climbed on to the seat and let go the chain which held the bicycle to the pole. Away we went down the grade, made by our own weight, and so swiftly that I almost fell off, and gripped the handle until the blood almost burst through my finger-tips. All I had to do was to sit there and work the treadles, stop at a given signal for the performers below and work back again. But, ye gods! when I looked down, my hair began to slowly rise and my teeth chattered so that I thought they would drop out. I know the few gray hairs I have came that day and upon that occasion, but with an effort I clinched my teeth and determined not to back out.

I was to make my *debut* that afternoon at the matinee performance, and in due time found myself bowing with three others in the ring, dressed in a suit of tights and spangles, borrowed from the sick gymnast's wardrobe. The next minute I was aloft standing on the narrow wire—how very narrow it seemed then!—waiting for the performers below to take their places. As the bicycle retained its equilibrium by the weight of the bodies on the trapeze, it was indispensable they should always be first on and last off, a rope slung from the pole ring above aiding them in their descent.

As I took my seat astride the machine and gracefully waved a hand to the audience, with an apparent *sang-froid* born of many years experience, my heart, or liver, tried hard to force an exit, and I honestly wished myself safe on *terra firma* again; but it was only the beginning. With a nervous hand I let go the chain that held us to the pole, and with both hands glued to the handle, started across the wire. I had often heard of jumping into space; this was literally *running* into it.

On my trial trip the gymnasts below had not tempted to rehearse any of their acts, probably knowing that I would back out entirely if they did; but once up there before the audience, and I was at their mercy. Of course I had often watched them perform from below; but the realization makes me shudder yet.

Two men and a girl were the artists and they certainly gave a startling performance. Hanging by their toes; swinging from the upper to the lower trapeze; jumping from bar to bar with a rapidity as startling as it was marvellous, caused the bicycle to sway from side to side with dangerous celerity and produce a sickening sensation that put the worst stage of *mal-de-mer* in the shade. The exhibition closed with a *coup de main* that sent my senses woolgathering, and from which I did not recover until I found myself safe back in the dressing tent.

On the last trip across, the lady was made to drop from her seat on the lower bar into the arms of one of the acrobats who hung in mid-air, suspended by his waistband, which was clutched by his comrade, who in turn hung by his knees from the bar above. Dexterously catching her by the right hand and left ankle, he literally turned her inside out, and holding her face downward in this position we slowly rode back to the starting point.

But the turn! Well, it was several hours before I recovered from the one it gave me, and small wonder either. The bicycle rocked wildly from right to left from the shock, and I almost lost my seat, said my prayers quickly, and wondered if my corpse would be greatly disfigured. Then, as the machine slowly righted, I mechanically worked the treadles, and in two minutes the ordeal was over, and back in the ring we were bowing ourselves out amid the *bravas* of the admiring audience.

SEVENTH EXTRACT.

I was paid the munificent sum of £2 per week (about ten dollars), and all expenses, to risk my precious neck in this manner twice a day. Shakespeare says truly, "What fools mortals be." My predecessor in this line used to make the exhibition still more sensational by bringing the machine to a dead halt in the center of the wire, and amid the breathless suspense of the spectators slowly raise his feet from the treadles, and stand with his head upon the seat and feet inverted directly above him, one of the acrobats meanwhile grasping the wheel and cable with an iron-like clutch to prevent its slipping. This used to bring down the house with a vengeance, and was a great card. I omitted it, however, for several reasons unnecessary to state here.

The first few days of this sort of life I passed in a highly nervous state; my sleep was haunted by visions of frightful accidents, in which I invariably saw myself carried out a mangled corpse into the dressing-tent on one of the hurdles used in the ring and covered over with a banner. It used to be a most edifying spectacle, and I usually awoke feeling greatly refreshed and in a delightful condition for the day's performance. But one can get accustomed to most anything, and this was no exception. I soon felt as much at home on the wire as I did aloft in the main-to'-gallant sail on ship.

Such is the perversity of human nature that I shortly found myself actually enjoying the swaying sensation and awaited impatiently the final *coup*, which was in reality a very risky piece of work and ought to have been cut.

For two months I traveled with the circus in this capacity, and also made myself useful in a variety of ways. Generally, when my act was over, I resumed my ordinary apparel, and after the clown had finished singing his comic songs, would pass around the audience selling "the clown's song-book, containing fifty different songs, the most popular airs of the day, price only a sixpence, with a picture of the clown on the cover of each book." They used to go off like hot cakes, but it was in the country towns that I managed to catch most nimble sixpences. Human nature is just the same in New Zealand as in Illinois, or any other place this side the water.

Living behind the scenes takes all the romance out of the exhibition. Truly "no man is a hero to his valet," and perhaps with good reason; the latter knows him too well, and has occasion to remember many things that do not always redound to said hero's credit. At any rate, I saw very little to admire in the array of talent gathered under the canvas we sported, and made few acquaintances among them; but there was one man that I greatly admired and with whom I contracted a great friendship.

He was the lion-tamer, a stalwart six-footer, muscular as an ox, and a giant in strength. He used to swear like a trooper upon all and any occasions, no matter how trifling, yet never in a passionate way, always as calmly as though pronouncing a benediction instead of a malediction. This was his greatest fault, and in every other particular he was a splendid fellow.

His performing lions were very much attached to him, and manifested their pleasure by various signs every time he approached the cage and spoke; but after all they were a treacherous pair, and he never dared turn his back on them when inside the den. In addition to his duties as lion-tamer, he was also elephant trainer, and "boss menagerie man," having full charge of the animals attached to the circus. Among them was a beautifully spotted tigress that he received when quite young, and which he was trying to break in for exhibition. She was a mean devil, however, and many were the deep scratches he had received from her, but finally an event occurred that gave him the complete mastery. It was at a place called Timaru, along the ninety-mile beach in the middle island of New Zealand, that the opportunity came, and I was an eye-witness to it, although an unwilling one, I must admit. The afternoon performance was over, and feeding-time had arrived, an event always heralded by loud-mouthed roarings and deep sullen growls from the hungry brutes who scented the banquet.

The tigress was in a particularly ugly mood on this occasion, and vented her spleen in a series of prolonged elocutionary efforts that I especially admired—from a distance. I was feeding my pet monkey, and watching the happy family in their many playful tricks, when a sudden shriek from one of the boys made me turn quickly, and I saw the tigress was loose. By some means she had torn up the floor near the front of the cage and managed to squeeze through, reaching in three bounds the mass of raw meat lying ready for distribution opposite her den.

In less than a minute I had shinned up the main guy of the center pole, and became an intensely interested spectator of the events that followed. The lion-tamer was feeding his pets with choice strips of raw beef, when he heard the cry, and taking in the situation at a glance, seized his heavy whip, loaded with lead, and without a moment's hesitation approached the escaped brute. For a second she cowed beneath his piercing glance, and shrunk back. That moment was fatal to her; before she could recover, the lion-tamer swung his weapon, and with a well-directed blow struck her directly behind the right ear, felling her to the earth. Following it up with several more, delivered with an equally telling effect, she was soon at his mercy, and lay a quivering, insensible mass of flesh. Then passing a strong cord around her neck and body, and aided by the assistants, who, like myself, had sought safety in flight, she was dragged over into an empty cage, hoisted up and securely fastened in.

All this took place in a remarkably short time, and was over before any outside assistance had arrived, when the tigress would have been the target for fifty bullets; but the coolness and daring displayed by my friend I shall never forget, and his courage can never sufficiently extol. Shortly after this another incident occurred of a very different nature, and although in nowise connected with the lion-tamer, was the means of causing us to part company, as I shall presently show.

In every department attached to the circus there was one man in charge who held more or less authority over the balance of the help employed in the same capacity, doing the same quality of work. For instance, there was the "boss property man," the "menagerie boss," the "boss candy butcher," the "boss canvas-man" and the "boss hostler."

The head of the latter department was considered quite a power, as besides having full charge of all the valuable ring horses and magnificent performing stallions attached to the show, he was possessed of no small skill in the veterinary healing art, and this was quite an item, considering the number of cattle under his supervision, and being constantly on the move, they demanded close attention.

But he was endowed with the ugliest temper that any mortal man was ever cursed with, and many a poor wretch has reason to remember his advent in the far-away latitudes of New Zealand. Upon the slightest provocation he would fly into a most fearful passion and vent his rage upon the unfortunate devil who had crossed his path, not alone with curses, but with kicks and blows, delivered with telling effect. He would snatch up the first thing that came handy, to use as a weapon, totally indifferent as to the result of his hasty action; indeed, the more severe the wounds he inflicted, the better he seemed to like it. I have seen him slash a poor trembling hostler, who perhaps was not currying a horse to his satisfaction, with a whip, and raise a wheal that his victim would carry for weeks. A bucket was his favorite weapon, and I could not but admire the accuracy of his aim, although deploring the result. I once displeased his lordship, and carried a bruise for six weeks between my shoulder blades, the result of a well-thrown curry-comb.

He lacked about two inches of six feet in height, had a massive pair of shoulders, and was built like a pugilist, so that very few dared retaliate, though many a one vowed vengeance; but as a rule his victims did not stay long under his wing, and he was continually hiring new hostlers, so that comparatively few of the help knew him as he was.

His tyrannical reign came to an end in rather a tragic manner, however, and he richly deserved his fate. We were showing at a small town in the interior of the south island when the event occurred, and the performance had closed for the night in a pouring rain-storm. Something had gone wrong with the trappings of one of the trick-horses that evening, and the ring-master made a complaint about it to the "boss hostler."

I heard the conversation, which took place after the show was over, and saw "Redney"—as he was nicknamed from his blonde moustache—stride over to the stock tent, cursing a blue streak, and threatening to kill the "black devil." I knew whom he meant by the latter appellation well enough, for it was the first man in his employ who had dared make a stand against his despotism, and was the hostler whose duty it was to groom the trick-horse and arrange its trappings for the ring. He was a half-bred Maori, a muscular, wiry-looking man, of perhaps thirty years of age, who had joined the circus at one of the "stands" in the middle island. Wrapping some spare canvas about me, as a partial protection from the pouring rain, I followed Redney to his quarters. The Maori was lying on a pile of hay just inside the tent, and by an unfortunate mischance, happened to be smoking. This was strictly against the rules about the stables, owing to the inflammable material scattered around, but nevertheless indulged in by all the hostlers surreptiously, though generally during the absence of their chief.

This was all that was needed to work Redney into a towering passion; he grew fairly livid with rage, and losing all control, seized an empty bucket, and brought it down with all his might upon the half-breed's back. The force of the blow broke the pail into pieces, and was enough to kill an ordinary mortal. But the Maori was tough, and though he howled from pain, he was eager for revenge—and had it.

A heavy stake-pin (such as was used for the large tent, and bound with an iron band) was lying near, and snatching it up, the dusky giant aimed a fearful blow at the tyrant's head, which fell right on the left temple, and Redney dropped like a log. Not content with this, he repeated his blows, and before any one could interfere, the position of "boss hostler" with that circus stood vacant.

Realizing his deed, the murderer did not wait for "back pay," but darted out into the black, pelting storm and disappeared, nor was much effort made to catch him, for in their hearts nearly all the witnesses to the deed mentally thanked him for ridding the earth of such a fiend.

This sickened me of circus life, however. Every time the trick-horse that had been the innocent cause of the quarrel came in the ring, I heard those heavy blows, and the dull thud as the stake came in contact with the quivering flesh, and within a week after the events just recorded I had quit circus life forever.

EIGHTH EXTRACT.

Leaving the circus at Christchurch, in the province of Canterbury, I determined to again try the sea, notwithstanding my recent severe experience; so went to Port Lyttleton, which is nine miles from Christchurch, and there made application aboard several vessels lying in port, for a berth. Being unsuccessful, and having saved a little sum from my earnings while with the show people, I secured passage in one of the Union S. S. boats about to leave for Dunedin, and two days later arrived at the latter town. Dunedin is one of the principal cities in New Zealand; has a population of about forty thousand, and by its numberless hills, very much resembles Kansas City in appearance.

I stayed here nearly two weeks without obtaining employment or getting a ship, and my finances were again deplorably low, when by a lucky accident

I was enabled to secure a berth on one of the vessels plying between New Zealand and Australia.

I was sitting one day down at the wharf, perched upon a mooring block, and in a very meditative mood was reviewing my immediate prospects, which were decidedly discouraging, when the steamer for Melbourne and Sydney came alongside and was made fast.

For two weeks I had boarded every ship that came in, and applied for a position unsuccessfully, and Melbourne especially was my objective point; so I mechanically made up my mind to interview the Captain or purser, and was preparing to go aboard, when I was saluted by a vigorous slap on my back, and heard my name loudly called.

Turning hastily, I saw a young colonial from Auckland with whom I had contracted an acquaintance when in that town. He belonged on the steamer just arrived, as he informed me, having shipped as brass-cleaner and lamp-trimmer the voyage previous. Dave was the only name I knew him by, but I remembered him as a very good-natured, obliging boy, and relating my situation to him, solicited his interest on my behalf for a billet on the boat. This he gladly promised to do, and as the vessel was only to make a short stay, he hastened aboard to intercede for me.

While I felt encouraged by his sanguine expectations, I had small hopes of his success, for it is no easy matter to get on these boats without good recommendations; so I sat dangling my heels against my perch until he returned.

By a streak of luck (or was it fate?) he had been successful; they had a large passenger list, were short handed in the galley, and on Davey's recommendation, I was shipped to fill the void. In less than half an hour I had my effects stored away under Davey's locker on the ship, and seated on an inverted bucket in the galley, was peeling "spuds" for dear life.

My intention was, when we arrived at Melbourne, to quit the ship at once, but from this I was dissuaded by my friend; indeed, when we reached there one of the understewards left, and being offered the billet, I accepted. From Melbourne we went to Sydney, and from thence to Auckland and Wellington, making the round trip.

By the time we arrived at the latter place I had made many friends on the ship, and enjoyed the life hugely. Our passengers had been remarkably generous and gay, and got up many pleasant entertainments, in which all the cabin crew were invited to join. On the return trip from Sydney to Wellington, the cabin passengers gave a very good upper-deck entertainment for the benefit of the Shipwrecked Mariner's Society. The Captain draped the after-deck very prettily with flags and bunting, the piano was brought up from the saloon, and the sailors, dressed in their best outfits, with their blue jerseys and white hats, were distributed here and there among the passengers, and made a very pleasing effect. The water was smooth, the moon at her full, and above us the clear Southern Cross, surrounded by a myriad of lesser stars, shone brightly upon the scene. The home talent was very clever, and all who did not take part in the program were delighted to contribute their mite and appear only as the audience. Vocal and instrumental music, both on piano and guitar, with recitations from popular authors, helped pass a very pleasant evening. I was put on the program as a representative of the understewards for a recitation, and gave them Will Carleton's touching ballad, "Betsy and I are

Out." Probably few there had ever heard of Will Carleton or his poems before, but this simple farmhouse ballad endeared him to all, and he was declared a true poet, inasmuch as he touched the heart.. After this the deck was cleared of the benches; a lady seated herself at the piano, struck up a lively waltz tune, and passengers and crew commingled in threading the "mazy."

Thus we passed the time pleasantly in fine weather, and I wish it could have been like this always; but as I write only facts, I must shortly present a far different picture. At Auckland and Wellington we began taking on passengers for Australian ports, and when we arrived at Port Lyttleton our numbers were swelled by a large delegation of ministers who with their families were going to South Australia to attend a conference. Altogether we had some seventy or eighty steerage passengers, and forty or fifty in the first and second cabin.

Our boat, the "Koturah," was not one of the best in the line, but it was a good stout vessel, and, having been recently overhauled and repaired, was considered perfectly safe. Our skipper, Captain Barret, although a young man, was very much liked in the service, not only for the excellent seamanlike qualities he possesed, but also for his amiable disposition.

The passage from Dunedin to the Bluff, at the southern extremity of the island, is a very dangerous one, and in consequence of the rocky coast, a vessel requires rather nice handling, especially as her course in some parts lies right between dangerous reefs on one side and several half-submerged rocks on the other.

We completed our passenger list at Dunedin and left there Tuesday afternoon, every one anticipating a quick trip to Melbourne, and retiring that evening full of hope at the bright prospect. I turned in at half past nine, very tired, and fell asleep immediately, being too weary to talk to my chum, Davey, whom I never spoke to again.

I awoke about five, and was dressing very leisurely, when I heard a rush of hasty footsteps on deck, and had just slipped on my vest, when suddenly the ship struck with a great shock against some obstacle, seemed to shiver all over, and then bumped continuously.

Putting on my coat I rushed at once on deck; it was then about 5.15 a. m., but though the stars still appeared overhead, a heavy mist concealed the land from view, for it was evident, by the repeated concussions, that the vessel had gone on the rocks. The engines had been stopped immediately, and reversed, but too late to be of service; we were fast between two nasty-looking, gaping rocks.

The scene that followed the first shock is something frightful to contemplate, and I feel sick at heart as I recall the dreadful sights. The bumpings continued incessantly, and the ship very soon began to fill with water, which poured in from a big gash made in her stern quarter.

Men, women and children rushed on deck, all in various stages of undress, screaming and yelling in a most heart-rending manner.

I have seen many strange and startling sights; but this was most dreadful! Captain Barrett, to his credit be it said, was very calm and collected. All hands were ordered on deck, and a boat was at once cleared for lowering. The steerage passengers, who came crowding up, tried to force their way in, but the Captain stood his ground firmly and ordered them back, swearing he would throw the first man overboard who attempted to crowd in. This had the desired effect, and in a little while order was partially restored.

By this time the boat was lowered, but no sooner had it struck the water than it was lifted right clear off the tackle and dashed against the ship's side, filling and sinking at once. The Captain then ordered the port boat to be cleared, it being much calmer on that side, and about six o'clock, nearly an hour after the vessel struck, the first boat was safely lowered.

Into this were placed the second officer, Mr. Riley, with four sailors and one passenger, who volunteered to go ashore for assistance. They had been absent about half an hour when Riley returned, saying it was impossible, on account of the heavy surf, to get within five hundred feet of the shore; but the passenger, a young man from Auckland, named Carey, had jumped overboard and swum safely to land, as he had been seen climbing the hill for help.

This was bad news, as it became evident no women or children, or in fact any but good swimmers, stood much chance in that direction, and we anxiously awaited the Captain's decision.

Meanwhile the women and children were all moved forward to the smoking-room on deck for safety, the seas making frightful sweeps over the after-part of the vessel. Another boat being lowered, the Captain called for volunteers—those only who could swim—and six of the steerage passengers pressed forward.

It looked then to us as though the vessel was the safest place, which I think accounts for the few who offered to leave.

The second boat was entrusted to the chief officer, with orders to get a line ashore from the reef if possible.

In this boat were the mate, the six passengers, four sailors, and (as I afterwards learned) little Davey.

They never came back. I did not know their fate at the time, but from one of the passengers in the boat, who escaped, and whose account of the wreck I afterwards read in the Melbourne papers, I learned they proceeded all right until within a few hundred feet of the shore, when a blind roller struck the boat right in the stern, making her turn a complete somersault and sending the occupants in every direction. All managed to get ashore, he stated, except little Davey, who sat on the same seat with him.

Just before the wave struck, Davey, who had been crying, said: "It's all through me; it's all on account of my bad luck that the vessel struck, for I carry it with me, wherever I go." Poor boy! these were probably his last words, for he never got ashore alive.

As he was a good swimmer, I think he must have been struck by the boat and perhaps stunned, for two others of the crew were injured in a like manner, although escaping with their lives.

The boat not returning, Riley was ordered to take three of the crew and three of the passengers (swimmers) and endeavor to pass a line ashore from the reef.

By this time it was about 10 o'ciock, and we had had plenty of time to view our position. We were ashore on a very dangerous reef, the swell being terrific at this point and making clean breaches over the vessel, carrying passengers and cabin-fixtures at every wash of the sea, and sweeping off everything that offered the least resistance.

NINTH EXTRACT.

I cannot conceive how we came to be so near in shore, but from what the Captain said later I think he mistook his position on account of the heavy fog, and not making due allowance for the southern swell, imagined he was much farther out. When the ship first struck, the second mate was in charge; the vessel was then running about ten knots an hour, a good average speed. The look-out, thinking he heard the breakers, reported to the second mate, who ran to call the Captain, instead of acting at once himself, valuable time being lost, that proved fatal. The Captain came immediately on deck, took in the situation at a glance, ordered the helm hard-a-starboard and the engines stopped and reversed, but before she could come round, on account of great headway she went on the reefs.

Mr. Riley having left the vessel the Captain gave orders for the women and children to be removed still further forward—from the smoking room to the forecastle, as her bows being wedged in the reef, it was by far the safest part of the ship. Twelve o'clock came, and Riley not having returned, Captain Barrett requested the cook to try and pass some kind of food forward for the crew and passengers as none had broken fast so far that day.

For this purpose a line was fastened around the cook and myself, and watching our opportunity we presently managed to steal aft, and fish up some crackers, cheese and cold meat; this was all we could obtain, and drenched through, we were hauled forward.

I do not believe any of us realized just then our imminent peril, for being so close to land and the fog having lifted, we could plainly discern the forms of the people on shore. It was not until Riley's absence was so prolonged that hope began to fail us, for the tide coming in the sea was much rougher and was pouring through the ship, so that we expected momentarily she would break up.

During a temporary lull we saw Riley trying to make up to us, but it was next to an impossibility for him to come alongside on account of the terrific swell, and with aching hearts we saw him, after repeated efforts, finally give up, and pull out to sea, where it was much calmer.

At about three in the afternoon, the Captain gave up all hope. Just as he was about to lower the remaining boats, a heavy sea carried away the longboat, cutter and dingy at one swoop, and we were completely at the mercy of the waves. I stood by the skipper's side hanging on to a stanchion when this happened, and he groaned out, "My God! what am I to do now? I have done my level best, and have no more boats available!"

These, our *dernier resort*, being gone, there was a rush to the opposite side, although for what purpose I could not exactly fathom. About twenty passengers were then hanging on to the taffrail, when a monstrous wave broke over them; the rail suddenly gave way under the enormous pressure, and without a moment's warning they were precipitated into the raging sea.

Such a frightful, unearthly yell of despair I never heard before or since, and can liken it to nothing. We were completely paralyzed by this appalling catastrophe, and could scarcely speak, the shock was so fearful. It was a matter of impossibility to render them the slightest assistance, for although two or three were seen struggling near the ship, the seas kept breaking over us with such violence, no one dared quit his position of temporary safety for an instant, and the poor wretches were swallowed up before our very eyes.

It was now about four o'clock, and our position was wretched in the extreme. All who had survived so far, had been soaked through by the salt water since early noon, and many of the women-folks had nothing on but their under-clothing and in some cases with only a ship's blanket wrapped round their damp night-dresses.

We were now collected in a huddled mass in the forecastle, the only, comparatively, safe place on the ship; in all about twenty persons, men women and children, that were left out of about one hundred and fifty souls.

These were one of the ministers, an elderly gentleman with long white beard, who sat completely unnerved and heart-broken, yet tried his best to offer spiritual consolation to the poor, shivering creatures around him; but who had lost wife, children and brother ministers in the last terrible wash of the sea.

With him, reclining at his feet, was a young gir of about sixteen, whom I had particularly noticed at Port Lyttleton, when she came aboard, with rosy red cheeks and bright laughing eyes. Poor girl; she had lost father, mother and friends in the remorseless deep, and was completely prostrated by grief. She, with three others, were the only females left out of twenty-five. Of these were the purser's wife; a young lady from Christ Church, N. Z., on her way to Geelong to be married, and a lady from Wellington, the latter being in company with a gentleman; all were saloon passengers. Beside these were the Captain, steerage steward, second engineer (with a broken leg), the purser, four passengers, two brothers (saloon) English tourists on their way home, the ship's carpenter, three sailors, myself and with me a little baby girl of five years, the chief engineer's little daughter, who himself was one of the first washed overboard; the little girl was in charge of the stewardess, but she being drowned, I had constituted myself her protector.

I do not pretend to say that I was any braver or even as brave as the rest, but I will say this: somehow from the first I felt convinced my time had not yet come, and this seemed to force itself powerfully upon me, and gave me a certain degree of calmness that I can account for in no other way.

Captain Barrett presented a most commiserating appearance, and his remorse must have been frightful, for had he, when the vessel first struck, ordered all the boats lowered and put out to sea to chance being picked up by a passing vessel, instead of trying to effect a landing on the inhospitable coast, no doubt many, if not all, would have escaped with life. It certainly was an error of judgment on his part, but I am not his judge, and he has gone to a higher tribunal to answer for all.

When the vessel first went on the rocks he had been struck by part of the steering apparatus across the forehead, inflicting a frightful gash, much blood flowing from the wound; this he had hastily staunched by tying a handkerchief around it, nor had he been able to attend to it since. Pale from loss of blood, and weak from constant exertion, his face streaked with the red fluid, bareheaded and with handkerchief grimed with blood and dirt, he was indeed a pitiable object. He did all that could be done by ordinary mortal to save the lives under his charge, and if he made a mistake, he did what he thought was for the best.

I can scarcely write what I now have to tell and many will affirm it to be incredible, but I call God to witness it is the solemn truth.

The purser was a young man of perhaps twenty-six, a very pleasant, affable fellow, who had been married only some seven or eight months, and was taking his young wife to Melbourne to her mother's, she being in very delicate health. It does seem rather strange that she should have made this journey in her peculiar state, but tempted by the previous beautiful weather and being anxious to be with her mother in her hour of trial, that lady not being able to leave home, she had at last made up her mind to make the journey. She was rather a weak, timid little thing, and the sad sights appeared to have made a powerful impression on her, but we were scarcely prepared for what follows.

At 4:30 p. m., one of the sailors, lashed to the foremast above, suddenly shouted "Lights! lights! A boat in sight!" Many at once rushed on deck, holding on to whatever came handy, and expecting instant rescue.

I looked at the Captain, but he shook his head despairingly, and indeed my own sense told me no boat could possibly approach anyway near the treacherous rocks to be of assistance; and so it proved.

After trying in vain to beat up toward us, she was compelled at last, for her own safety, to bear out to sea. When the lights presently disappeared, and all knew there was no further chance (for this had been the only hope to buoy us up since the loss of the small boats), the scene became utterly indescribable.

With a fearful scream the purser's wife suddenly fell senseless by the foremast, round which we had congregated, and in the midst of the raging storm and seas that broke over us incessantly, gave birth to a child, which, of course, was dead ere it came into the world.

As soon as we had recovered to some extent our

bewildered senses, several pressed forward with the intention of carrying the poor lady below, but in this they were frustrated by the husband, who, poor fellow, had seemed utterly paralyzed with horror at the awful spectacle. With a yell which told us reason had fled, so wildly demoniacal was it, he forced the horror-stricken spectators aside, picked up his wife's form as though she were a mere feather; and before we could stay or speak to him, leaped overboard into the boiling, raging ocean.

God in heaven! such a fearful, blood-curdling sight never was before, and for a moment we forgot our own misery in the contemplation of a greater. But the waves now made it an impossibility to stay on deck, and we cautiously crept back to the forecastle below, intending to keep the sad scene a secret from the surviving females if possible, but alas! it had been witnessed by the Wellington lady who had stood clinging to the companion ladder, and had plainly seen the double tragedy.

Uttering a ghastly shriek, she fell upon her face and prayed God at once to kill her for her wickedness; in wild ravings she called upon her companion to put an end to her existence. From her many incoherent mutterings we learned that she, with the gentleman accompanying her, had each left home and relatives, and in guilty consort were fleeing from an injured husband and deserted wife. In vain her guilty paramour tried to soothe and pacify her; she refused his offerings with loathing, and spurned him from her. After a while she became somewhat calmer, but continued her moanings, which were dismal and heart-breaking enough.

God knows we had enough misery without this final touch, and were completely dumb and appalled at this final *denouement*. It was now about six o'clock, and we were unable from the growing darkness to see each others' faces, small comfort as that was. Some few, however, had wax matches, and these were burned far into the night.

The men were mostly without coats or hats, those articles have been long since parted with to the women folks who had perished in the waves. I was without coat or hat, even my vest I had given away; but so were my fellow-sufferers, so I would not complain; indeed, I could not, for the prospective bride (poor girl, destined to be the bride of Death only) had on my coat and hat, forced upon her shivering form, and my little curly-headed charge was enveloped in my vest, not that I am so large, but she was so very small.

The boat was now fast breaking up, and we scarcely expected to survive the night. At twelve o'clock, midnight, by the captain's watch, after being on the rocks all that terrible eternity of a day, we bade each other Good-by! and after a touching prayer by the good old minister, committed ourselves to God.

The water was then breaking through the timbers into the forecastle, and it became necessary to seek other quarters. The vessel was gradually settling and as a last resort we were compelled to take to the rigging. This we finally succeeded in doing after incredible labor, the captain taking charge of the young girl. Carrying her in his arms and followed by the white-haired old preacher they were finally made fast in the foretop. The second engineer, a brave, true-hearted man, managed to crawl to a place beyond the reach of the waves, although suffering tortures from his unset broken arm. I, with my protege tied around my waist, her little arms clasped tightly round my neck, succeeded in reaching a position near the captain, and close by, supported by the fore-cabin steward, a young Tasmanian, was the unfortunate Geelong lady. What became of the wretched couple from Wellington I know not, for when I left to creep aloft the man was vainly endeavoring to persuade his companion to move; my impression is he stayed below with her, and they perished together.

Meanwhile, the people on shore had lit huge fires, which we could plainly see, and several forms were discerned flitting about. I am sure we were apparent to them, for the glare of the fire shone plainly upon the wreck, but it would have been madness to venture out to us; a boat would have been smashed upon the rocks instantly.

TENTH EXTRACT.

Cold, hungry and wet to the skin, many shrieked and craved for death to relieve their sufferings, but had not sufficient courage to jump into eternity; just so long as the timbers kept above water so would they, and they fought for life till the very last.

The matches were long since exhausted, and about two o'clock Capt. Barrett, who was immediately below me, cried out, "God help us all, we are going fast."

This was only too evident, for even by the fitful glare from shore we could plainly see the upper deck was completely submerged. What I felt I can scarcely describe; but I know I made many good resolutions for the future in case my life was spared, for somehow I still had the notion strong within me that I should be saved; but how? I had not the least idea. There certainly was no immediate prospect.

And now the little girl who had been remarkably good began moaning for her papa, and cried piteously for something to eat. I own that I cried like a baby with her, only softly to myself.

At three o'clock the waves washed over us as we sank lower and lower, and we were face to face with Death trembling on the verge of the Unknown. The good old minister had long since dropped exhausted into the sea, his lashings having parted, and there were only about eight in all left to linger on.

We were now level with the water, and it was plain all was over. Slipping my lashings, I began to prepare for the worst, for although I knew a swimmer had small chance in such a sea and among the jagged rocks, still I was bound to make a bold fight for life.

Just as I was about to mount still higher, hoping to escape by clinging to the mast, in case all was not submerged, an immense wave struck me, and, loosing my grip, I was dashed off from the rigging into the foaming billows.

Down! down! I went, meantime holding my breath, and trying hard to retain my senses, for in the midst of all, I could still argue to myself. When

I arose I struck wildly out and had not taken half a dozen strokes when my hands came in contact with a hard substance. I grasped at it, and finding it was large and apparently capable of sustaining my weight I clambered up, and found to my joy it was a cumbrous sea-chest, floating about securely fastened and perfectly water tight.

But great Heavens! My little baby girl was gone. How, when or where she was parted from me I have not the slightest conception; for having had her arms about my neck so long, I imagined until I struck the chest that I held her safely and that she still clung to me.

The terrible shock, when I struck the water, must have parted us, and in the struggle for life I had not noticed—being half dazed—her disappearance.

Poor little thing! it was certainly all for the best. Had she lived, her lot would have been a hard one; her father and mother both gone and she friendless and alone, so God in His mercy took her home to rejoin them.

I myself, however, was by no means safe, for

the waves tossed me up and down like mere cork. Blinded and half-choked by the briny water, it was a hard matter to hang on to the chest, and had it not been for a cord that was fastened securely round it and which I gripped with the strength of despair, I certainly must have been washed off.

Fortunately for me, when I fell, it was on that side farthest from the reef, so that instead of being carried on to rocks, where I would have been instantly dashed to pieces, I was gradually being washed out to sea, and the farther I got from land the calmer it became. To this circumstance alone do I attribute my escape, for now, if I could only manage to stick to my strange life-preserver, I had some show of being picked up by a vessel.

As soon as it began to get calmer I endeavored to pierce the gloom for a sight of the ill-fated ship I had been so forcibly parted from. But I could not even hear the breakers, and must have drifted out a much greater distance than I deemed possible in the time.

What strange thoughts then took possession of

me. All the wonderful escapes from shipwreck that I had ever read or heard of, rushed across my memory, and I especially remembered Dr. Haines' escape in Chas. Reade's *Simpleton*, a book I had only lately finished reading.

I wondered whether I should drift about as he did and if the exposure and privation would affect my mind similarly. I pondered and wondered over this for so long that it is a marvel to me now I did not go crazy then and there, but by God's mercy I was preserved from such a fate.

It must have been about three o'clock when I was parted from the wreck so unceremoniously and I had been tossed about, the sport of the waves some two or three hours when a certain grey streak in the east foretold the gradual approach of daylight.

Never in my life did I welcome the dawning of the day more than on that memorable morning, for in the past twelve hours of darkness, had been crowded the misery of a lifetime, the memory of which will exists in my brain never to be effaced while life lasts.

With what heartfelt joy and gratitude did I behold, as soon as the darkness was fairly dispelled, a schooner under full sail standing up directly toward me, so that she would pass easily within hailing distance. I could scarcely contain myself for joy, and barely kept from plunging headlong into the sea, in order to reach her sooner.

Never did a vessel travel so slowly, in my fervid imagination, and fifty times I fancied her bearing off in a contrary direction, at which thought I would be almost ready to drop off my faithful chest in despair.

But, thank God! she came within hailing distance at last, when, with one hand clutching the cord, and with the other waving aloft my limp and briny shirt, I shouted and gesticulated until weak with the exertion.

But that was of small account; I was heard and seen, and a boat was at once lowered, manned by four stout sailors. In a few minutes my immediate troubles were over, and I found myself safe, although very weak, on the broad deck of the vessel, in company with my thrice blessed chest, which the sailors had towed along with us.

I found her to be a small trading schooner, bound for Melbourne, with a cargo of sundries. Her skipper proved to be a kind, good-hearted man, who, after hearing what little I had to say, insisted on my going at once to bed, which I was only too glad to do.

Nothing could have exceeded Captain Wilson's kindness to me, and I shall ever remember him, and also his crew, for their exceeding indulgence to me during the voyage to Melbourne.

When picked up, all I had on was my blue serge trowsers and grey undershirt—my linen one I discarded when I saw the boat lowered—so that my condition was a forlorn one. When the chest was forced open—which was rather a difficult matter, so firmly was it fastened—it was found empty, which accounted for its singular buoyancy. The owner had evidently taken out the contents and bound it thus securely, with an ultimate view to the use I had made of it; but, poor fellow, he had never profited by his efforts.

I presented it to one of my rescuers, the sailor who had lifted me into the boat, and by whose orders the chest had been towed along. He swore to keep it as long as he lived, in remembrance of the event.

Before we reached port, the skipper made up a purse for me, and to which all the crew contributed, so that when we dropped anchor in Hobson's Bay, I found myself possessed of quite a neat sum, which was duly laid out in purchasing clothes and other necessary articles. I was very weak and feverish when we entered Port Philip Heads, but managed to go ashore with Captain Wilson and get rigged in a new outfit of store clothes; and having a few other purchases to make, I promised to meet him in an hour at the vessel office of his line, on Collins street. But I had overestimated my strength, and very shortly after my kind friend left me, I felt a dizziness in my head, the buildings began to grow larger and larger, and assumed all manner of queer shapes, until I imagined they were trying to crush me to pieces. I remember taking a sharp turn toward an open common, away from the buildings, and staggering ahead as fast as my weak knees would carry me; then I knew no more for some days.

When I recovered my senses, I was lying in a low bed, in a large airy room, where there were several more cots ranged in a row on each side where I lay. A woman, apparently a nurse, was at the other end of the apartment administering medicine to a patient, who seemed to be somewhat fractious, and who answered my sharp exclamation by hastily quitting her occupation and coming to my side. In response to my anxious looks, she told me I had been very ill with the fever, and must not talk. Then, taking a bottle from a stand near the bed, she bade me drink, which I mechanically did, and in a short time was fast asleep.

When I awoke, it was dark, but I heard voices near me, and presently a gentleman approached the bed, and put his hand on my forehead. Then a voice which I recognized as belonging to the nurse, said: "He was awake this morning, Doctor, and appeared quite sensible like, but I gave him his medicine, and he went right to sleep again."

I concluded this must be the hospital surgeon, for I had made up my mind that I was in some public institution, from the number of beds in the room; so, opening my eyes, I asked the Doctor where I was, and how long I had been sick. He told me I had been very ill for two weeks; that I had been found near the grounds by one of the keepers, in a fainting condition, and had been raving mad for nearly a week; that I had talked of nothing but horses, and monkeys, and trick ponies, and occasionally bursting out in some comic song, from which they concluded I was an attache' of some circus.

Evidently I had been living over my old life with the circus, and had not dwelt on my late terrible experience at all, for which I felt thankful, as I was too weak to bear questioning. Putting my hand to my head, I found it bare, and seeing my look of dismay, the doctor said he had been obliged to cut my hair all off to cool my head during the fever.

I also learned that I was in a private insane asylum, having been admitted through the surgeon's kindness, and that it was about six miles from Melbourne, so that I must have walked on for some time in my insane desire to escape from the falling buildings, when first taken sick.

ELEVENTH EXTRACT.

For nearly two weeks after recovering consciousness I continued an inmate of the asylum, and through the friendship of the house surgeon was very kindly cared for by the attendants. During convalescence I was allowed to wander through the incurables' ward, where the poor demented but harmless creatures passed the long, sad hours of the day. It was a beautifully appointed garden, filled with richly colored flowers and tropical plants, and abounding with cool, vine-covered arbors and rustic seats—everything that would please the fanciful eye and fantastic imagination of its insane frequenters.

Here I became acquainted with some of the highest personages of both the past and present ages, and also made fast friends with many of the leading characters in Bible history. My earliest introduction was to a grand-looking, imposing, white-haired old gentleman, who fancied himself to be God Almighty. He was always in search of his dear and only son

Jesus Christ, and when I first entered the garden he came straight toward me and inquired if I were not that illustrious person. When I undeceived him he appeared much cast down, and said, as he passed a thin, delicate hand over his massive white forehead, that he was afraid his son did not know the way, or he certainly would come and take him away from such a place. He had been an inmate for over five years, the keeper told me, and went crazy over the loss of his wife and only son, who were on their way from England to join him at Melbourne, but were shipwrecked almost in sight of Port Phillip Heads. He used to take me by the hand and introduce me to all the notabilities of the place, so that before I left we were quite intimate. One day, when sitting alone with him on one of the pretty rustic benches, he took a piece of folded paper from his pocket, and looking anxiously around to see if the keeper were watching him, slyly slipped it into my coat pocket, and in a whisper told me to read it when alone. Thinking perhaps it was some complaint he had written out, I took the first opportunity to read it. On the outside, traced in a neat, legible hand, was this inscription:

"——God is love; Staff Sargeant William Topping—God Almighty—Melbourne."

Inside was written the following:

"God is love and Motherless. Staff Sargeant William Topping, God Almighty. Two is company, three is none. Dear brothers and sisters, be kind, be kind to the breath of life. Bless the Queen and all little children. I mend clocks and watches, hearts and souls, and breathe life into the new born babe. I am God Almighty, this is my home. There is no place like home, where the birds are singing gaily, and there is no place like home. Do not love the devil; he is my worst enemy."

I insert this merely to show how disconnected such a mind can get, and how pitiful and awful is the loss of a grand intellect. This man, I was informed, had been one of the leading merchants of Melbourne, and a member of the Victoria parliament, where he was a brilliant speaker, but was now a hopeless, incurable lunatic. I think those days of my convalescence were among the saddest of my life, as I witnessed, and moved about in daily conversation with, so many just such pitiable wrecks. To enumerate them singly would only be telling what any one who has visited an asylum for the insane has no doubt seen, so I will pass over this experience as briefly as possible.

One nice old gentleman used to take me by the arm every morning, gravely feel my pulse and look at my tongue, then mutter a few words and pretend to write a prescription, which he would gravely hand me, with a grand gesture of the arm. He was once one of the most skillful surgeons in the colonies, the keeper said, but the use of opium had utterly destroyed his brain and reduced him to his present state; and his relatives had been forced to place him there for safe keeping, as it was impossible to watch him at home; and so I might go on, *ad infinitum* but I desist.

All this time, as I gradually grew stronger, I yearned for news from the outside world, especially relating to the loss of the "Koturah." With a strange reticence I had said nothing to my friends regarding my identity with the wreck, and as they had no suspicion of the true facts, I did not care to open up the old wounds, which close questioning would have revealed;

so as they believed me to be merely a wanderer from a circus troupe lately exhibiting at Melbourne, I let them remain in ignorance.

But one day, while lying on a sofa in the matron's room, I chanced upon some newspapers which had been left for my amusement, and glancing through an old copy of the Melbourne Argus, came upon the following, which instantly attracted my profound attention: "An Extraordinary Story! The captain of the 'Early Dawn' has a strange story to tell, which, were it not known that he is a man of undoubted veracity, could hardly be credited; but beside the gentleman's own word, the story is fully corroborated by the officers and crew of his vessel. Captain Wilson says: 'On Saturday, the — inst., while standing direct on our course for the Bluff, the lookout reported man overboard off starboard bow, flying signal of distress. Had just come on deck and at once ordered a boat lowered and the unfortunate fellow was picked up and brought on board. He proved to be a youth of about eighteen, probably 5 ft. 6 in. tall and of rather stout build; he was afloat on a seaman's chest, which, being water-tight, had sustained his weight and saved his life.

"'In answer to our inquiries we ascertained he was one of the crew of the unfortunate vessel which was lately wrecked off the southern coast of New Zealand, holding the position of under-steward on board. He was reticent about giving particulars, and seemed somewhat dazed by grief and horror. From what little he said we inferred the scenes on the lost ship were too heart-rending to bear repetition, for he shuddered, and averted all mention when the subject was introduced.

"'He promised, however, to make a full statement on reaching Melbourne, and, as he was very weak and sick during the balance of the voyage, we abstained from all further questioning. Upon arriving at Hobson's Bay, we made up a purse among ourselves to enable him to purchase a shore outfit of clothes, as he had nothing on when picked up but common serge trowsers and singlet.'

"And now comes the most singular part of the officer's statement. Captain Wilson, resuming, said:

"'I brought him to town here, and, while I went to report myself at the office, he left me to make some purchases, promising to meet me at the company's office within an hour. I was on hand promptly, and waited some time, but the boy did not show up, and I have not set eyes on him since. As he was not at all strong, I am afraid he was taken ill, but what has become of him I cannot say, for in spite of every effort I have been unable to discover his whereabouts.'

" This ended the captain's remarkable story which is true in every particular. The boy is undoubtedly one of the crew of the ill-fated Koturah and what is more to the point, is certainly the only survivor with the exception of those few who escaped in the first and second officers' boats. His statement would no doubt throw great light on the subsequent scenes which transpired on the vessel, for as he had only been in the water three or four hours, he must have been one of the last survivors who clung to the rigging. The only suspicious thing about the statement is the name given by the youth. .It corresponds with none of the names appearing on the list at the company's office, but may be accounted for in this manner: The youth was probably shipped at one of the many ports of call, and, in such case, would not be entered excepting upon the ship's books, which, of course, were lost. The spectators on shore, who remained until the vessel had totally disappeared, say they could plainly see forms in the rigging until nearly three in the morning, when the vessel disappeared entirely from view, and a last despairing cry was all that was heard from the perishing wretches who had thus far survived.

"It is highly important this young man should come forward, not only on account of the additional news he can give, which would be eagerly read by the relatives of the deceased passengers, and the public in general, but also to appear before the court of inquiry, now in session, where he would prove a valuable witness."

In another column I read:

"A reward of twenty pounds is offered to the survivor of the Koturah who arrived in this city with Captain Wilson, and will be paid him by the proprietors of this paper, on condition of making a full statement of the loss of the vessel, together with particulars occuring on board, &c., &c. He is also requested to communicate with E. O. Barrett, Ballarat, Vic., brother of the unfortunate captain."

Further on I read of the recovery of the captain's body, which had been washed ashore, together with a number of others, some of which I recognized by the description. Among them the unfortunate Geelong lady, the body of the second engineer, that of the venerable minister, and the poor little child, whose life I had so vainly endeavored to preserve. With the exception of those in the first and second officers' boats none had been saved except myself. The second officer and crew had pulled out to sea in safety, and had been picked up by the vessel whose lights we had seen and counted so much upon. Those with the first officer escaped by swimming through the surf. I then read of poor Davey's untimely death and last words. His body was recovered next day, badly bruised and disfigured, as were indeed nearly all the bodies that came ashore.

Imagine my feelings upon reading the foregoing. All the past rushed in upon me, as the old wounds reopened. And the paper was two weeks old. The court of inquiry was by this time all over, and the verdict long since given. Why rake up the bitter past? It was all settled and over, and so I determined to leave things as the court had decided.

I thought it strange at first that the surgeon had no suspicion of my identity. But the clothes I wore when they found me insensible were new and of shore cut; my eyes were haggard and my cheeks pale, while my shorn head helped to alter my description not a little. Then, I had purposely given an assumed name, so that, all things combined, they were enough to deceive the most skeptical, and my new friends had certainly no reason to doubt my former occupation, as my ravings were sufficient proof to allay any misgivings upon that subject.

And so I stayed on for a few days longer, when, my strength being nearly restored, I told my friend, the surgeon, I would go to Sydney, where I had friends. This was not wholly true, as I knew but one person in that city and he but a chance traveling acquaintance. Still I wished to avert all cross-questioning, and thought this the better way. He was very kind, and through his influence obtained a passage for me on one of the steamers that ply between Melbourne and Sydney. Despite the melancholy atmosphere which I had lived in for nearly four weeks, I was loth to leave the asylum (to me it had been a veritable refuge) and my strange companions, but I wanted to get away from Melbourne, and was eager for a change.

On the boat I became acquainted with a young colonial, who was a purser and steward combined on one of those small trading vessels that coast about the Australian Islands. His boat sailed from Sydney to Levuka, the British settlement in the Fiji Islands, and, learning I wanted a position, he offered to take me as assistant steward on the next trip.

TWELFTH EXTRACT.

This offer I gladly accepted and in less than two weeks I was installed in my new position and enjoying the delightful tropical breezes only to be found in the latitudes of the Southern Pacific ocean.

Among the passengers was a very intelligent half-breed native of Levuka, with whom I contracted a friendship, and who proved to be a very interesting companion. He was thoroughly posted on all leading events connected with the history of the Fiji Islands and having lived almost entirely with the English residents (his father had been employed at the English embassy at Levuka) spoke our language fluently. When his father died he had the grace to will to his illegitimate offspring a two-thirds interest in a large coffee plantation which was located only a few miles from the town.

All this I learned at odd intervals during our trip from Sydney, and when we arrived at Levuka, we were on such friendly terms that Viti (my friend's name) invited me to spend a week or two with him on his plantation. As I was still quite weak from my recent sickness, I was glad to avail myself of this offer, and knowing the vessel did not return for three weeks, I obtained permission from the captain to absent myself for a fortnight.

I was scarcely prepared to see such a state of civilization existing at Levuka, although my friend had given me a general description of the place previous to our arrival; but the churches, the hotels, and the warehouses along the wharf, had such a very modern and civilized aspect I could scarcely realize that only a few years back the place had been the haunt of cannibals and savages.

The road to Viti's plantation led through a delightfully fertile valley and I was again astonished at the evidences of cultivation everywhere abundant. Cocoanut trees, palm trees and beautiful ferns also flourished extensively, while beneath our feet luxuriant flowers, of that rich coloring only to be seen in tropical countries, grew profusely. As I watched the gaily-tinted birds flitting above us, and felt the warm southern sun penetrating my linen jacket, I felt a delicious languor stealing over me and thought of Monte Cristo's experience with the hasheseh, and wondered if his sensations equalled mine.

Viti was married to a half-breed native, who, like himself, had been raised in a white family and she, with an old native woman who did the housework, constituted the family.

Here I spent two happy weeks and as the time drew near for me to leave, I was almost tempted to relinquish all claims on country and friends and stay forever. But before bidding Levuka and Viti adieu, I must relate a peculiar experience which came within my ken.

I had been on the plantation a little over a week when one night I was awakened by hearing loud moans as of one in pain. Presently Viti rushed into the room and implored me to go to his wife while he ran for the native doctor, who lived at the further end of his plantation.

Hastily donning my *pajamas* I made my way into the next room and there, attended only by the native beldam, lay Viti's wife on a low cot still uttering the same loud cries that had awakened me.

It was my first and only experience in this line and I think all my readers will be apt to pardon me when I affirm that I was frightfully nervous and "rattled." But I soothed and held the poor woman to the best of my ability, and with the assistance of the ancient cook managed to quiet her; but before Viti had returned, the Doctor's presence was unnecessary; his wife was sleeping peacefully and the old woman held up a fine little boy to Viti's delighted gaze.

As a compliment to me, my friend declared the the boy should bear my name; so by reason of this I have the honor to stand god-father to one of the rising generation and future citizens of Levuka, Fiji Islands.

I took an affectionate farewell of my namesake, Viti and his wife. The most highly cultured and civilized European could not have entertained me more hospitably, or kindlier, than did this Fiji half bred native and we parted with mutual regrets. Perhaps some day I may return to pay my god-son a visit and carry him the long delayed "silver-mug;"

but whenever I do I am very sure of a warm reception and with the knowledge that I am freely welcome to partake and share of all that he and his parents enjoy.

With renewed health and spirits I went back to my ship, and the following week sailed out of the reef-bound harbor. My duties were by no means arduous, and I have reason to remember the trip back to Sydney as one of the pleasantest periods of my life.

Our captain had been a whaler in his younger days, his cruising grounds having been principally in the Southern Pacific, between New Zealand and the Fiji Islands. Whales are not so common there now as then, but forty years ago it was a very prolific station for a whaler to cruise in, and big money was made in a short time.

Our skipper's stories related mostly to the peculiarities and cannibalistic propensities of the Fijians, varied occasionally by a long yarn about a pull after a "spermer," with the incidents pertaining thereto. Often on a calm summer evening, after nine o'clock tea, when the silver moon shone placidly across the long expanse of water, and the Southern Cross glittered brightly overhead, I used to join the captain, mate and purser, as they sat chatting and smoking by the wheelhouse, and listen for hours to the yarns our "old man" used to spin.

Like all sailors, he was very much given to stretching a "p'int," but then he would never spoil a yarn for the sake of a trifling inaccuracy of fact. He used to especially relish telling us of a long, weary pull after a whale, and night coming on, the whole boat-load taking refuge on one of the islands in the Fiji group until morning. Surprised by the savages, all made a rush for the boat, into which they hastily scrambled and pulled out to sea, hotly pursued by the natives in their canoes. The captain, however, in the rush and darkness was left behind, and climbing a cocoanut tree, he hid in the foliage. It was lucky he did, as his comrades were overtaken, ruthlessly murdered and eaten, almost underneath the place where he was stowed safely away.

When he arrived at this stage of the yarn, our captain used to turn to me and remark upon the gusto with which an old toothless native seized upon the fat tempting arm of the harpooner of the boat and with an epicurean smack prepared for a delicious morsel. It happened, however, that the spear-thrower had been so greatly addicted to the use of tobacco that his entire system was thoroughly impregnated with the nicotine. At the second or third mouthful the old warrior dropped the arm in disgust, and temporarily retired from the feast—the tobacco being too much for him.

I suspect this part of the story was an addendum by the captain for my especial benefit, as he used to roll his eyes wildly at this point, and pull savagely at his pipe.

Then he told us how next day the balance of the ship's crew came in shore, hunting their lost comrades, and the cannibals being gone, the captain descended from his perch and was taken back to the ship, where he told the sad story to his sorrowing shipmates.

Allowing for local coloring, I have no doubt the story was true, as it is a notorious fact that the natives in some parts of Fiji do kill and eat human beings. Indeed, while I was at Sydney I read of the massacre of the crew of a small coaster, the remains of the unfortunate victims being discovered some weeks after by an adventurous trader.

However, we were in no mood to criticise or doubt any of our skipper's stories, as that would have been like killing the goose that laid the golden eggs, and shutting off our yarns entirely.

We enjoyed and believed them, (at least I did) and were all sorry when we entered Port Jackson Heads and cast anchor in the bay. My strength was then entirely restored, and the vessel being laid up for repairs, I was ready for new adventures.

It was then I caught the gold fever, which at that time was invading the conservative old city of New South Wales, and I could not rest until I had found a kindred spirit, who was ready and willing to go "up country" with me on a prospecting tour.

We both knew about as much of mining as a three-year-old colt, but that made no difference to us. We were bound to go, and investing our scanty finances in a few necessary articles, started out on foot for our new Eldorado.

All went well until the fifth day out, when we

began to strike the sandy desert through which we must pass before the auriferous deposits could be reached, and here my companion was taken with the sand blight, so that it was impossible to proceed, his eyes being so inflamed that he could not open them.

We were forced to go into camp, despite our anxiety to advance, and for nearly a week I constituted myself cook, nurse and doctor to the expedition; but my comrade, instead of getting better, grew worse, and I was compelled to sell our entire stock of tools and camping outfit in order to raise money enough to convey my chum back to town. I was fortunate in meeting a party of miners, outward bound, who were ready to purchase, and to them I sold everything but our blankets. A stage coach made irregular trips to the nearest mining camp, and I was lucky enough to secure two seats on the return route. The fare was pretty high, and nearly bankrupted me, but it had to be paid. My companion was totally unable to return as we had come, and was suffering tortures.

He was very fortunate in gaining admission to

the hospital when we arrived at Sydney, and there received the attention his condition required. But as for me, with money all gone and wardrobe somewhat dilapidated by the recent journey, I was in a sad state. My friend, the purser, with whom I had recently sailed, had left about two days before I returned, and I found no vacancies on any of the ships lying at the circular quay.

I was in this condition when I formed an acquaintance with a street fakir, one of those clever artists who contrive to make a living out of nothing. He had a scheme that promised to give us bread and butter and as I was hungry I did not stick at trifles. His great forte as an artist was in imitating bird calls by means of a small tin contrivance called by courtesy a bird whistle, which, inserted on the tip of the tongue between the palate and the roof of the mouth is used to emit certain peculiar sounds that are supposed to resemble the warbling of birds.

His idea was to make these whistles and sell them in the Saturday night market for a small compensation. As neither of us had a penny, and credit was out of the question, the scheme did not appear very feasible at the outset but I was soon enlightened. My share in this joint operation was to go around to the various leather finders and harness-makers in the place and beg small scraps of refuse leather, after which I was to select several discarded empty tin cans, such as are used for preserving fruit, and meet him with my spoils in Cook's Park, near the great navigator's statue.

My new friend was a great genius. In the course of four or five hours, with his few crude tools, of which on old jack-knife was the most important article, he had fashioned between thirty and forty bird whistles "so easy and simple that a child could use them."

The next day was Saturday and at seven in the evening we repaired to the market grounds. This Saturday night market is one of the institutions of Sydney and is mainly patronized by the poorer class, who imagine bargains may be picked up here cheap. One can buy almost anything from a baby carriage to a bedstead at the booths and stands, which are to be met at every turn, and interspersed with these are small side-shows, quack medicine doctors crying their wonderful "cure alls," lemonade venders, oyster-stands and the ever-present electric-try-your-nerve artist. These attractions are all rendered brilliant and inviting by the aid of a multitude of oil-lamps, which shed a peculiar flare on the grounds and emit a most uninviting odor to one not accustomed to the scene, but which to its frequentors is one of the main charms of the market.

We paid our small entrance fee, obtained by making a sale outside, and carrying an empty box, to serve as a stand, we entered the grounds and securing a likely position near a popular quack-medicine doctor (?) we soon commenced operations.

Whilst I mounted a friendly stump and extolled the simplicity and beauty of our wonderful bird-whistles, my coadjutor stood beside me and trilled forth roulade after roulade in a manner that would have done credit to the most finished nightingale and that attracted a crowd of admirers in a very few minutes.

In half an hour all our whistles were sold and after dividing our profits we found ourselves possessed of a fair sum to last us through the week. The following Saturday we repeated our success, only to a greater extent, as we had printed forms explaining how to learn the various calls, which we distributed, gratis, to every purchaser of a whistle. We were highly elated over our good fortune and began to think of starting a manufactory on a small scale for our whistles and sell them wholesale to the trade, when alas! our air-castles were rudely overthrown by the Vandal's hands and we were forced to find a new outlet for our refined tastes.

But ere I go further, let me confess what I had previously but half guessed at. As a matter of fact no one could ever learn to use our bird-calls unless possessing a positive knack in so doing; apt trickster as my comrade was it had taken him years to become the finished artist he was.

The third Saturday saw our sun go down, or to speak more correctly, saw our lamp knocked out, and we were escorted out of the market followed by a score or more of howling colonials whose British blood was up and who demanded back their "thruppence" for the "beastly thing, that wouldn't blow ye know?"

Thus perished in its infancy an enterprise that might have grown into colossal dimensions and have been one of the chief industries of Australia. I felt sorry for our victims, but I had to eat some way, and that was my only chance.

THIRTEENTH EXTRACT.

My partner in this adventure was a man with a history, who had seen life from a variety of standpoints. He was an American by birth and had been in the colonies but a few months when I met him, having arrived at Sydney only a short time before me, after a protracted stay in Java. He rejoiced in the particularly euphonious and somewhat peculiar title of "Seldom Seen," which was the only name I knew him by. He was the purest specimen of the genus tramp ever engaged in "drilling" the road, and when in the States had been a perfect terror to the conductors and brakesmen along the U. P. road.

No one could steal a ride, "jump the brakes," crawl into a "tool-box" or force open a box-car as neatly and easily as he, and it was from his daring propensities in this direction and ability to render himself scarce and invisible to the eyes of the hawk-eyed brakesmen on the Union Pacific railroad that he obtained his alliterative cognomen.

He was a long, lean, hungry looking chap, with big, staring, grey eyes, a shock of red hair and a stubby growth on his chin, of the same dirty brick color, which generally looked as if it had been trimmed with a very dull jack-knife but of which he was not a little proud.

He possessed an easy, good-natured disposition, was full of ready wit, when brought to bay by an irate conductor, and could sling such choice bits of profanity at his natural enemies, the brakesmen, or "brake jerkers," as he termed them, as to completely overwhelm even those hardened creatures.

The incident that I am about to relate was the main cause of his leaving the Pacific slope and crossing the ocean. The details I picked up from time to time as he grew more or less communicative and I have endeavored to present them in as connected a form as was possible under the circumstances.

The boon companion of Seldom Seen in all his escapades and adventures, was a short, stumpy little fellow, who answered to the pleasant and suggestive appellative of "Jimmy-hit-the-road-a-welt," called "Jimmy," for short. For three years they traveled together, in every direction that railroads had penetrated, and in that time had visited nearly every town of any size in all the States and Territories in the Union. When one was seen hanging around a freight train or loafing about the yards at any railroad terminus, it was tolerably certain the other was not far off, for like David and Jonathan they were inseparable and their staunch friendship for each other was the one redeeming quality they possessed.

When Seldom Seen had three fingers crushed and his right thumb cut off between two couplers, one bitter cold day in December, Jimmy it was who took him to the hospital at Cheyenne and actually went to work in a coal yard in order to keep his sick comrade supplied with such delicacies he might fancy and to pay the sum necessary for his care. On another occasion in the summer time, when on their way to Utah, Seldom Seen risked his life by a daring leap in order to assist his partner who was in distress.

They had boarded a freight at Laramie, one evening at dusk, and Seldom Seen with his usual recklessness had launched himself beneath the car, to his favorite seat on the brakes, while Jimmy hung low on the iron ladder at the rear and was partially hidden between the two cars.

When approaching Summit, and while the train was running about six miles an hour, one of the brakesmen discovered Jimmy on his perch and stealing along the roof of the car dealt a cowardly blow with all his force upon the poor fellow's head. Jimmy dropped like a log between the cars, the forward wheels of the rear freight just missing his neck and passing over his right arm close to the elbow.

From his cramped seat beneath the car Seldom Seen could not see this inhuman act, but he heard his comrade's despairing cry as he dropped, and with an utter disregard of consequences hurled himself between the wheels and actually lit in the ditch along the track without a scratch.

Hastening back he found his partner lying senseless on the ties and picking him up bore him as tenderly as he could to a deserted section-house which was fortunately only a few yards distant.

For six weeks Seldom Seen nursed his mutilated

companion, making daily excursions to the neighboring ranches for food and at one time going clear to Laramie for a doctor, whom he succeeded in inducing to accompany him back, after infinite exertion, to dress the injured limb.

Poor Jimmy lost his arm, however, and never seemed to recover his former spirits. He drooped away like the jackdaw of Rheims, when under the cardinal's ban, and gradually grew weaker, until at the close of fall he resembled only the ghost of his former self and was even thinner than his partner.

Seldom Seen's conduct under these circumstances was heroic. He bore patiently with his comrade's irritability and trying moods, when growing convalescent; worked on a ranche near by, in order to supply him with proper food, and at night cheered his lonely hours with stories of former adventures and such amusing instances as he calculated would best please him.

But as the winter approached, Jimmy grew worse; he had received some internal injuries, which hitherto had been quiescent. The cold weather brought on a troublesome cough which racked his form and produced such severe pains in his head that he could scarcely sleep.

With the first fall of snow, Seldom Seen was obliged to resign his work on the ranche and take his sick partner to Laramie where the latter was compelled by his comrade to visit a doctor.

The result of this interview was not submitted to Jimmy, for obvious reasons. In reply to Seldom Seen's anxious questioning, the physician replied that Jimmy's only chance of recovery was in seeking a warmer climate, as, if the cough was not stopped, it would certainly result fatally, precursory symptoms of consumption having already made an appearance.

Winter was now fairly set in and the snow lay deep on the ground, yet Seldom Seen determined to go through to California with his patient. Having no money, but one course lay open, the usual orthodox method, adopted by all the profession, viz: get "sprung in" in a box-car, and take the chances of getting as far as Ogden, without being discovered, after which, by easy stages, make the balance of the trip as far as Sacramento.

A sudden spell of warm weather brought Seldom

Seen's plans to a focus; a marked car was selected having breathing holes at the rear, and with the help of a friend, both managed to crawl beneath the raised sliding-door, into the car, without being detected.

An old army blanket for covering; two large bottles of water and several loaves of bread were stowed carefully away in the car to guard against any mishaps from breakage, and just as daylight began to peep in through the iron grating at the rear, the cars moved slowly out of the yard and both breathed a long sigh of satisfaction as the journey to the west began.

It was no novel experience to either; but at this period, and taken in midwinter it was scarcely pleasant or safe, and only the exigency of the case had nerved Seldom Seen to make the attempt.

The first day Jimmy seemed quite pleased at the contemplated change and was even cheerful at times, occasionally breaking out into a comic ditty the burden of which was, "You kin bet yer life we'll get dar, halle-halle-halle-hallelujah."

But Seldom Seen was obliged to repress this merriment, for fear the brakesmen, who were constantly passing and repassing the roof of the car would overhear it and discover their presence; so Jimmy finally fell back on his blanket, and quietly listened to the dull rumbling of the wheels, or the subdued murmur of his companion's voice, telling some thrilling story of bygone experience.

Once Jimmy's hacking cough almost betrayed them, a sudden paroxysm seizing him just as a brakesman was passing overhead, but at that instant came the shrill whistle for "down brakes" and the sound was drowned.

Towards night on the second day, it began to grow much colder and poor Jimmy shivered like an aspen leaf, despite the protecting warmth from the blanket, which Seldom Seen had wrapped round his comrade's form.

Presently Jimmy began to whimper, and waking his companion from a sound sleep accused him of cruelty and meanness, for subjecting him to such inconveniences when he might just as well have stayed at Laramie where they were at least able to have a good fire.

Seldom Seen, the patient fellow, bore it all very submissively and tried to soothe his sick comrade's peevishness as he best knew how, but all to little effect; Jimmy refused to be pacified.

As the evening wore on his chills grew more violent so that Seldom Seen began to grow nervous over the result. Finally, as a last resort, he took the poor, shivering wretch in his arms, wrapped the blanket securely about him and holding him close to his bosom tried to impart some of his natural heat to the poor wasted frame of the once robust Jimmy.

Meantime a furious snow-storm had set in which raged with terrific fury all through the night, and with the first streak of morning light, Seldom Seen, from the opening through the grating, saw the train was laboring with difficulty along the track, the snow being piled up on each side and clogging the wheels at each revolution.

Fortunately, with the snow, the weather moderated so that Jimmy ceased to complain of the cold but the poor fellow was rapidly growing worse, and about noon his mind began to wander so that he imagined himself back in his mother's home in the green mountains of Vermont, his poor, feeble mind reverting in its last efforts to the place that gave him birth.

"Marmie," said he, in a whisper, clutching his faithful partner by the wrist, and falling into the endearing vernacular of early childhood, "don't fret about me, you know I mean well enough and if I'm a little rough at times, it ain't 'cause I don't love yer. It's dull and lonesome down here and I want to git out and see the world and I must go: but I'll come back, dearie, I'll come back again."

His mind was evidently dwelling on the time he first left his home and a fond mother—the mother he would never see again and the home he would never re-visit.

Large tears slowly welled out of Seldom Seen's eyes, as he again took the weary, worn-out tramp in his arms and listened to the low murmurings that were quietly breathed forth.

He was now turning back again from his wanderings, journeying again to the woman who had toiled and worked, early and late, for her restless boy who had fled the nest as soon as his wings were sufficiently strong to carry him away. Seldom Seen bent low to catch the dying words: "Yes, marmie, I'm coming, I'll stay this time for g—" here a violent fit of coughing checked further utterance and when it was over Seldom Seen held in his arms a corpse, and poor Jimmy was home at last.

Wrapping the lean, wasted form of his dead partner in the faded blanket, Seldom Seen reverently crossed the one remaining arm over the breast and gave a great gulp as he laid the body carefully out on some boxes in the center of the car. Henceforth the world was a blank to him; his partner would not be there and he was alone with his sorrow.

To add to his distress he discovered the cars had ceased running; the storm continued with unabated fury and it became evident towards night the train was abandoned.

The storm raged nearly six days. At the end of that time, a sudden thaw set in and the train men were able to renew their duties. A brakesman climbing over the deserted train discovered a dirty brown muffler tied to the grating of one of the cars and evidently for the purpose of attracting attention. Summoning his comrades, they broke open the car door and there found the dead body of Jimmy-hit-the-road-a-welt and lying by its side the insensible form of Seldom Seen.

He was carried into the caboose, brandy forced between his clenched teeth and after a time he recovered sufficiently to ask for "Jimmy," relapsing immediately into unconsciousness.

The boys were very good to him when he finally managed to tell his story, and he was taken to Ogden where some kind people buried his partner and obtained a pass for him to San Francisco. There he staid some time and gradually grew stronger, but he determined to leave America for awhile, so shipped on a sailing vessel for Java from whence he drifted to Sydney, where I made his acquaintance as before mentioned, and learned this little episode connected with his career.

FOURTEENTH EXTRACT.

After the "bird-whistle" experience I did not see much of Seldom Seen, who had associated himself with a small side-show in the capacity of "canvasman;" but as I had a few shillings in my pocket, left from our joint mercantile venture, my position was not quite so dubious as it was previous to making his acquaintance.

Sydney, as a commercial city, is far behind its rival, Melbourne, the bustling capital of Victoria; but no prettier location could possibly be found in the colonies to live in. The bay of Sydney is accounted among the finest in the world for its natural beauties and excellent anchorage; and could one sail in from Port Royal Heads on a fine summer day, and view the delightful green banks on each side of the bay, dotted here and there with handsome white residences, which, half hidden among the trees and foliage, form a charming background to the already very striking picture, the question as to its claims would be ceded without argument. From the Heads to the Circular Quay, the scene that meets the eye is one full of beauty, that once seen is never to be forgotten; and I shall always remember the trip I took to the Heads and back, on the little steamer, "Ly-ee-Moon," as one of the pleasantest spent days of my life.

Flowing past the city, the bay becomes the Parramatta river, and standing on one of the many hills of Woolloomooloo, a suburb of Sydney, a fine view can be had of the river for some four or five miles, the channel at this point being famous as the praticing and racing course of all the noted Australian oarsmen. About a dozen miles above are the celebrated orange groves of Parramatta. Some of the trees at Pye's Grove are fully forty feet high, and when I was there the lower branches of a great number were bowed almost to the ground by their heavy cargo of fruit. Pears, apples, and the fragrant guava fruit also, are grown here in great abundance, and I can vouch personally for the delicious flavor of the fruit.

Botany Bay is now very unlike the place where England once transported her convicts, but is a veritable garden of Eden, where the colonists flock in great numbers on Sundays and holidays to listen to the delightful open-air concerts, drink home-brewed beer and roam about the beautifully-kept grounds.

The Botanical gardens of Sydney also add to the charm of the place, and in them I spent many a pleasant hour. Magnificent tropical flowers and rare specimens of flora are to be seen there, while the collection of wild animals and birds indigenous to that country is equal to a whole volume of natural history; and being free to the public, the grounds are naturally liberally patronized, especially on Sundays, when thousands turn out to enjoy the green parks, beautiful shade trees and glorious flowers.

One day, in company with a young "middy," I went down to visit the dry-dock at Cockatoo Island, and there saw the old "Alert," of Arctic fame. (Which, by the way, was recently tendered by the British government for our use in the proposed search for the Lieut. Greely expedition.) She was undergoing repairs, being then engaged in the revenue service, and was fitted up as a gun-boat, for coasting purposes. We went down in a row-boat, and my friend having a "permit" to visit the island, we were entitled to go aboard and examine her, which afforded me no small amount of pleasure.

Recalling the perils she encountered in her icy voyage, reminded me of my aspirations in that direction two years previous to this occasion. I was then crazy to join the Arctic expedition in the Jeannette, and in conjunction with an acquaintance who courted the Muse at one of the smaller theaters, dispatched an appealing letter to Capt. De Long, asking to be allowed to ship with him. I remember one of the strong points I made in it (and done at the suggestion of my friend,) was the fact of my being able to entertain the ship's company during the long winter evenings by various means in my power, and which ought to be an extra inducement for him to ship me. In view of this I learned a great many sleight-of-hand tricks, comic songs and other accomplishments of that order, all taught by my obliging artist acquaintance; but to no purpose, as I soon learned. When I think over that letter now, I am forced to smile at the absurdity of my proposition; when I read over the answer I received from Capt. De Long, and remember that the brave but unfortunate officer has been but a short time buried in his native country, I am very thankful it said what it did. Perhaps the letter I received from him may not be out of place here, so I give it:

No. 150 West Eleventh Street,
New York, April 1st, 1879.

Mr. S. T. Clover,
Chicago, Ill.

Sir: Your various letters have been received. In reply, I would state that I have room in the Jeannette for nobody but her officers and crew. These must be seamen, or people with some claim to scientific usefulness, and unless you can be classed with either party, I cannot possibly take you.

Very respectfully,
Geo. W. De Long,
Lieut.-Commanding Arctic Str. Jeannette.

This effectually settled all desire to take part in an Arctic voyage just then. Yet, when I stood aboard the Alert in Sydney harbor, not knowing De Long's fate, I may have sighed to be with him. At present writing, however, this insane freak has totally disappeared, and the late commander of the Jeannette has my best thanks, although, poor fellow! he is not in a position to appreciate their worth.

My shillings having rapidly dwindled during this short relaxation from the regular "hustling" routine, it behooved me to recuperate in some direction, so noticing in the *Sydney Herald* an advertisement for a canvasser by the Cologne Ink Manufacturing Company, I applied for and obtained the billet.

I was instructed by the manager to first call, with my samples and cards, upon the principals of all the schools and Colleges in and about Sydney and endeavor to introduce the celebrated German "Kaiser-Tinte" writing fluid, to their particular notice, and to this end, I was furnished with a number of small sample bottles which were to be left on trial at the various schools I called at.

Overhauling the directory, I made out a list of twenty-five or thirty names and started off, my pockets lined with a couple of dozen homœopathic doses of "Kaiser-Tinte." Most of my intended victims were "high-church" professors and their schools were under the patronage of the church in whose parish they were located. Thus, beginning with St. Andrew's on Pitt street, I visited St. James, St. Leonard's, St. Mark's, St. Phillip's and all the other blessed saints in the calendar, but without obtaining a blessed order; and totally discouraged I finally introduced myself to the "head-master" of the Hebrew School on Castlereagh street and tendered my minature samples for his inspection, at the same time handing him a circular. He eyed the latter suspiciously over the edge of his gold-bowed spectacles and, glancing at my shabby clothes, said: "Young man, uf you don'd get oud I gife you in charge to der bolice; I know you; you vas a shneak-thief; Solomon, show him oud." Solomon was a dull, heavy-eyed Jew, with rather big hands and large, heavy feet, who acted as servitor to the institution. He proceeded to handle me rather roughly, which aroused my ire, already near unto bursting from the doctor's speech, and just as we reached the outside gate, my progress having been accelerated by several rough pushes from Solomon's too ready hand, I turned round, drew the cork from one of my sample bottles, let him have the contents full in his face and then darted out into the street and ran for my life.

Solomon did not pursue however; his build would not allow of very rapid transit, and I was safe, but as

I neared George street an unlucky stumble threw me off my balance and I fell heavily on the stone coping of the pavement. I was not hurt much, but the fall had broken all my sample bottles and the ink quickly soaked through both pockets penetrating to my skin, leaving its indelible traces from my hip to below the knee on one side my body. My clothes were barely presentable before, now they resembled the rough proof of a badly-constructed war map; the suit was light in color and the "Kaiser-Tinte" was not. Solomon was amply revenged.

This experience sickened me of the ink business, however, and when the agent asked what had become of all my samples, I called attention to my "half-mourning" suit, whereupon he sarcastically observed I had better apply for a position as book-keeper since I could sling ink so successfully. This was a cruel thrust, but then these colonials are young yet and when they grow older and wiser, will, I hope, learn what bad form it is to hit a man when he is down. I confessed my incompetency to act as his agent, so without any regrets on either side, we parted.

A day or two after this mishap, I strolled out to

see the races, at Randwick, given under the auspices of the Australian Jockey Club, and while there became acquainted with one of the "book-makers" who was well-known upon the turf and had liberal patronage among the sporting men. As the races were to continue for several weeks, and being very busy, this gentleman had the kindness to engage me as his clerk to record the bets, make out the slips and figure his percentage. The pay was good, the work easy and my conscientious scruples allayed by the thought that only stern necessity had compelled me to accept his offer. When the races ended, I rejoiced in a new suit of clothes and a good sum saved from my salary, beside having a five-pound note presented me by my employer, who had been particularly fortunate in his book-making, while I was with him.

This streak of luck had introduced me to more comfortable lodgings, for soon after my engagement I removed to a small hotel on Pitt street, kept by an American, who had resided in the colonies several years. Here I formed the acquaintance of a dapper little Frenchman named L'Estrange, an aeronaut by profession and instinct. Next to a journey to the arctic regions, nothing could have pleased me better than a trip up in a balloon; consequently, having ulterior designs upon the professor's good-will, I cultivated his acquaintance assiduously.

The 24th of May, being the anniversary of Queen Victoria's birthday, the colonials, who are very patriotic, especially when a holiday is the outcome, resolved to celebrate the happy event by a grand *fete*, to be given in the public domain in the evening, the programme to consist of speech-making, fireworks, music and dancing, the whole to conclude with a grand balloon ascension given by my friend Henri L'Estrange. I had made up my mind to ascend with him.

It took a long period of coaxing before I gained the point, but he finally consented, and like any other idiot, I was supremely happy—for a time. As the day drew near I was conscious of a growing nervousness on the subject, induced no doubt, by a visit to the public library, where I read up all the authorities on aerostatics, that I could find, the French statistics being especially interesting—and discouraging to a novice.

It was too late to back out, however, and the evening of the twenty-fourth saw me in company with the professor trudging over to the grounds. It was a beautiful star-lit night; there was no moon, but the atmosphere was singularly clear and bright, and objects could be discerned for some distance away. Henri had previously made arrangements about having the balloon filled with gas so that when we arrived the huge silken bag was surging to and fro, as if anxious to escape from the thraldom it was subjected to, by the dozen ropes that pinned it to the earth.

There was considerable delay in starting owing to the inferior quality of the gas, which, while it filled the folds of the bag, yet lacked sufficient power to be of the required buoyancy, and I fervently hoped that L'Estrange would be obliged to refuse me at last on this account. But no; he motioned me into the car, gave the signal to let go, and in a grand blaze of fireworks we shot quickly up.

Those of my readers who have ridden on a very fast water-power elevator to the top story of a first-class building for the first time in their lives, may be able to form some little conception of the feelings I experienced as we mounted skyward. For two or three minutes I was unable to speak or think, but grasped the wicker car in an agony of suspense, and inwardly vowed that if I ever got back to terra firma not all the gold of a Vanderbilt could tempt me to leave it.

We had ascended about a hundred and fifty feet when my senses began slowly to return, and I caught sight of Henri looking fixedly across from his seat on the opposite side of the car; he was laughing—and at me. This braced me up, and I plucked courage from the very desperateness of the situation, to grin back, but it was a ghastly attempt, I am sure, for the market was scarcely ripe that produced it, seeing which L'Estrange desisted, and called my attention to the fact that we were descending.

The gas was unequal to our combined weight, together with the car, and we settled slowly but surely, finally landing within a hundred feet of our starting point. The ropes were quickly made fast to the unwieldly mass, and with a thankful heart, I jumped out and stamped firmly upon mother Earth, with inward satisfaction at the speedy termination of my aerial voyage.

The professor was not satisfied with his share in it however, and sent notices round to all the papers that he would make another attempt the following evening. The fact was duly advertised and a big crowd gathered the next night to see him off. This time he went alone. The gas was still bad, but, rather than disappoint the people, Henri had the car detached, secured himself in the net-work of the balloon, and, in this manner, had the hardihood to ascend.

The "Empress of the Night" soared grandly up; L'Estrange meantime, with cap in hand, waving an adieu to his audience. He did not rise very high, but gradually veered south, toward George Street, the crowd following on foot, and eagerly watching his progress. Barely escaping a net-work of chimneys on one of the larger buildings of that street, the balloon continued sinking, and the crowd stood ready to help æronaut out the moment he touched the ground.

Just as everything pointed to a speedy and safe

descent, the balloon passed by the open window of a large building on George Street, where a lighted lamp stood on the table. The escaping gas ignited, exploding with a terrific noise, and poor L'Estrange fell like lead upon the roof of a small shed which stood about a dozen feet below.

Fortunately he had escaped being singed by the flames, but he struck in such a manner that his arm was doubled under his body, and a broken wrist was, luckily, the worst result.

I was effectually cured of Arctic aspirations by reading of DeLong's hardships; I was also cured of aeronautics by this personal observation.

FIFTEENTH EXTRACT.

I had been absent from Chicago nearly nine months, and during all that time had only received two letters from home, my movements having been so erratic it was impossible to locate me. In my last letter to the folks, written and mailed at Honolulu, I had requested an answer to be sent, care of general post-office, at Sydney, N. S. W., and for some time had been anxiously expecting it, as I especially wished to learn the address of some near relatives who resided somewhere in the colonies.

A day or two after the balloon episode, while walking down George street I noticed the flag was hoisted from the post-office building, a signal that the mail-steamer had arrived. In answer to my inquiries at the general-delivery window, the clerk rapidly ran over the pile of "C's" and handed me out four bulky-looking missives, bearing the familiar U. S. stamp on their faces. I greedily seized them, and made a hasty exit from the building, going over to the Botanical Gardens, where, under the shade of a friendly palm-tree, free from all curious eyes, I eagerly perused the contents of my letters.

"News from home!" Who has not felt his pulse quicken when, thousands of miles from friends, and in foreign countries, he opens his correspondence to read the interesting details, penned by a loving hand, of the hundred and one things that have happened during a prolonged absence.? Of friends married, of friends dead; of business troubles or advancements, of wonderful personal adventures, and narrow escapes from accidents; of sister's latest successes at school, and the baby's last extraordinary bright saying. All these events in their turn were duly recorded, intermingled with many loving wishes for the wanderer, and "God speeds" for a safe return. Never in my life have letters received a warmer welcome than on that occasion, and he who has journeyed far away from loved ones at home will appreciate the feelings that took possession of me at that period.

I learned, among various other items of interest, that the very near and dear relative of my mother lived with his family at Adelaide, South Australia, and to whom she had already written of my advent in that part of the globe, so that they would be ready to receive and welcome me when I put in an appearance.

Having experienced considerable more of roughing it in these far-away islands than I felt was due me, I determined to take the other tack for a time, and enjoy the comforts of a nice home and the companionship of cultured people, for such I felt assured my relatives would prove to be; so two days after receiving my letters I left Sydney on the steamer City of Adelaide, for Adelaide, via Melbourne.

My late engagement as clerk to the "bookmaker" had left me in good funds and I was well supplied with clothes, so that I was under no apprehension as to my personal exterior, and with economy I could make my money last until I returned to Sydney, from which point I intended shipping to London.

Two days and nights on the water landed me at the Queen's wharf in Melbourne, and as I wanted to see something of this city before leaving Australia—not having been able to on my previous visit—I concluded to stay over a day or two before proceeding on my journey to South Australia.

Melbourne has a river that even a Chicagoan would take exception to. It is called the Yarra, and is a veritable cess-pool, emitting the most offensive smells, that in warm weather are positively unbearable; yet despite this fact, much of the water used for drinking purposes is obtained from this very river after being filtered. It is termed locally, "Yan Yean" water. I drank some once by mistake, and it made me very sick.

The public buildings of Melbourne are very beautiful edifices, and a credit to the government. The city hall and new post-office buildings, constructed of clear white polished granite, especially attracted my attention and admiration, not only on account of their superior construction and beauty of architecture, but by their massive size and imposing appearance. The streets are wide, cleanly kept and well paved, but the sewerage is very bad, the gutters after a heavy rain-storm often becoming miniature torrents; and it is on record there that upon one occasion, after a severe storm, a young child fell from the sidewalk into the gutter and was drowned before assistance could be rendered.

There is one bad feature of this city that must strike the most casual observer, and that is the great number of demi-monde parading the streets, even in the principal thoroughfares of the town. After nine in the evening, continuing until nearly midnight, Bourke and Swanston streets are literally packed with these *nymphs du pave*, who strut boldly up and down the wide pavement, their favorite beat generally extending from the city hall to Bourke street and return.

The sheep herders from "up country" are their favorite victims, these poor devils generally falling an easy prey to their wiles. A sheep tender will come down to the city once or twice a year with his accrued savings, earned by a long and tedious exile at his "station" in the bush, and deliberately proceed to squander them away in a series of "drunks" and companionship with lewd women.

The favorite plan is to deposit their money upon arriving in town with the proprietor of the hotel where they intend boarding during their stay, and make him their banker. The boniface keeps them well supplied until there is barely enough left to pay the board bill and carry them back to their solitary home in the bush, when having run their rope, the fun (?) is ended for the season, and they go back to save up for their next visit, when the same program is enacted.

The jaunty little steamer "Aldinga" carried me from Melbourne, ploughing its way through the tortuous Yarra to Sandridge, the port of Melbourne, where all the "deep-water" vessels lie at anchor in Hobson's Bay. On our way to the Heads we were startled by a terrific explosion, evidently proceeding from a large gun-boat stationed in the bay. We were too far off to turn back, but knew from the commotion that something serious had happened; and upon arriving at Adelaide learned that a boat's crew from the turret ship, while engaged in placing loaded shells for submarine-defence experiments, had been blown into atoms through the carelessness of one of their number, who had touched the electric battery and fired the torpedoes before giving them time to pull to a safe distance. It was a sad occurrence, and caused much comment, the colonial press as a body denouncing such dangerous experiments as foolhardy unless practiced under the particular charge of an experienced electrician.

I was not at all disappointed in the estimate I had formed of my Australian cousins; they made me very welcome, and each individual member of the family vied with one another to entertain me during my protracted stay of six weeks, I was received as one of the family from my first appearance, made much of by my fair cousins; as a brother by the male portion and a son by the parents; nothing, in short, could have exceeded the kind and considerate attention I received, and I take this opportunity of extending my warmest thanks for their many kindnesses to one whom they had never seen before, but who happened to be the son of his mother.

Yachting, cricketing, trips to the neighboring summer resort at Glenelg, (which latter place is the Coney Island of South Australia); picnics, moonlight excursions, dancing and card parties; all combined to make a very enjoyable visit and one that I shall never forget. I made desperate love to all my fair cousins, from the saucy miss of fifteen to her sweet, sedate sister, ten years older, in fact took all fair advantage of my ties of consanguinity that could be admitted and was very proud of the privileges it gave, even if it did make some of the Adelaide boys, admirers of my fair cousins, fearfully jealous during my stay.

I appreciated the pleasant lines into which my lot had fallen, the more, because of the harsh contrasts to which I had been subjected previously, and I should very much like to dwell longer over this visit, but being afraid that some of my more critical readers will object to enlarging further upon it I am forced to be brief.

It was with a heavy heart that I said farewell to Adelaide. The little city is charmingly situated, located as it is in a beautiful valley, bounded on both sides and rear by a chain of mountains, while in front flow the bright blue waves of the Southern Pacific. But my funds were getting low; I was still a gentleman of leisure, and having lavishly opened my purse at every opportunity I considered it advisable to beat an honorable retreat while the course was clear. Not a word about "circus" had I mentioned; not that I had attempted to deceive but because I did not wish to offend the tastes of certain of my relatives' particular friends, who would have looked upon me with holy horror at the bare mention of the word.

The trip back to Sydney was a slow and tedious one; head winds harassing us all the way. During the voyage I was initiated into the mysteries of a game called "Nap," which is as great a favorite in the colonies as poker is with us. It is somewhat similar to Pedro, but much more exciting. The captains of the steamships plying between Adelaide, Melbourne and Sydney used to join the passengers in the game at every opportunity, but once, while a captain was engaged in its seductive charms, his vessel collided with another, the passengers and crew barely escaping with their lives; and after that the managers of the steamship line issued a peremptory order forbidding all commanders to play at any game while in charge of their vessel, instant dismissal from the service following any infringement of the rule.

Our captain used to sit in the smoking room on

deck and watch the game with wistful eyes, for on account of the bothering head winds, we made slow progress and time being heavy on his hands; but he did not dare take a hand, as the mates on each boat were very keen for promotion and would have reported the delinquent skipper without fail.

I arrived in Sydney just in time to see the "positively last performance of the 'Great American' Circus,'" my former acquaintance of New Zealand and arena of various foolhardy exploits. I had made several warm friends among the troupe and they appeared very glad to see me again, but their stay was short, and three days later I stood upon the circular quay and watched the Pacific Mail steamer move slowly away from her moorings, on her way to the heads, *en route* to San Francisco with all the circus people on board.

April 21st, Thursday: Again I am left alone; it seems as though my entire wanderings had been spent in making friends and losing them, just as they were growing particularly interesting, but I suppose it is the traveler's usual fate that one must gradually get accustumed to, so I must grin and bear it.

Friday, 22d: Am getting tired of Australia and very homesick. Shall endeavor to ship on the next Orient boat that comes in as ordinary seaman or steward, the latter, if possible, as I doubt if I am yet strong enough for the hardships of life on the fo'castle again. This afternoon while walking down Pitt street found a small peculiarly-shaped key, evidently belonging to a safe; shall keep it and see if the owner advertises for it.

23d, Saturday: Verily, "God helps those who help themselves." This morning's *Herald* contained advertisement for lost key, finder to call at Queensland Bank. Manager of bank described and proved key as his property and tendered me compensation for trouble. Refused offer, but asked him for letter to the manager of the Orient Steamship Company, explaining that I wanted to ship. Promised to use his influence and told me to call again the next Saturday.

The week passed slowly enough. My appetite at this time was positively voracious, yet on account of my scarcity of funds I was obliged to restrict myself to one meal per day, usually eating a three o'clock dinner. To shorten the time between meals as much as possible I would read after dinner at the public library until ten o'clock, then borrow an interesting book, go to my room and read until three or four in the morning, then sleep until two in the afternoon, thus saving the expense of breakfast, and making dinner serve as supper also.

Saturday came, and as soon as I dared I repaired to the bank to interview the manager. He was as good as his word, nay, better; for he had spoken personally to the manager of the steamship company and the latter had promised to give me a letter to the captain of the incoming vessel, that being the extent of his authority; but it satisfied me, for I felt sure that with a recommendation from the agents I should have no trouble in getting a berth. Nor did I. The captain indorsed my letter and bade me see the chief steward and let him read it. The fates were propitious, one of the under-stewards had met with an accident which disabled him from work, and I was at once shipped to fill the void.

SIXTEENTH EXTRACT.

I was assigned to the duties of under-steward or "general servant," and if I had an easy time on shore during the preceding weeks, I more than made up for it by my first week on board the "Chimborazo."

I used to think life before the mast as ordinary seaman aboard the Pacific mail boats was pretty hard work, but it was mere apprenticeship to my present duties.

While in port we were all kept very busy scrubbing the paintwork on the main or saloon deck, cleaning the silverware, getting in stores and holystoning the main deck, that being entirely under the steward's charge, and apart from the sailors' duties. The latter job was not begun until after coaling, when the boards were fairly black with the searching dust that had settled everywhere. My back ached for nearly two weeks over this pleasant task, and I do not think

I shall forget my initiatory performance in this line if I live a hundred years.

Getting in ice, however, was the final *coup*, that nearly sent me adrift. As the homeward course lay directly through the very hottest latitudes, this was a very essential part of the commissariat, and to keep well, the ice had to be very closely packed. Four of us were detailed to enter the freezing compartment and store the ice away as it was swung down to the lower deck. The room was long and narrow, so that as the congealed lumps began piling up, it soon became necessary to lie at full length upon the frozen blocks, and with our picks stop up all the crevices with broken pieces, in order to make it pack well. I occupied this enviable position for nearly four hours, lying alternately upon my back and stomach with only a potato sack between my thin serge pants and the chilling ice. When we had finished, the doctor ordered us a double dose of brandy, and told us to put our wet clothes in the dry room and "turn in."

Our sleeping quarters were designated by the boys "Glory Hole," and was known as such throughout the ship. It was situated just forward of the main saloon on the deck below, and was separated only by a thin partition from where the passengers' baggage lay stored. It was a dark, dreary hole fitted up with a number of wooden bunks or "pews," as they were dubbed, and lighted by an oil lamp, which hung from the center of the room.

Between twenty and thirty stewards were forced to sleep in this stifling atmosphere, night after night, such being the only accommodation provided for them on the ship; but they were mostly young fellows inured to hardships, and I heard very little complaint while my lot was cast with them.

From the moment of my introduction to the "Glory Hole" I had been christened "Yank" by the wit of the mess, an illiterate genius called "Scully," so named from his filling the position of scullery boy in the cook's kitchen, his duties being to clean the various pots and pans used in the culinary department. He could neither read nor write, but was the brightest specimen of native British humor I ever happened across. Shipped at London, it naturally followed that my messmates were Britishers and mostly cockneys, too, so that my nom de voyage stuck to me throughout the tripe, and was indeed the only name I was known by.

From Sydney we went to Melbourne, where more passengers and stores were taken aboard, the latter consisting principally of poultry, bullocks, hay, grain, etc. It was what we termed a "field day" among us, the latter expression being a pet phrase with the boys when any extra work was on hand. Our next and last call at Australian ports was at Adelaide, where we completed our list of stores by taking in a quantity of flour, and also shipped several more passengers. I wanted very much to go ashore and say farewell to my cousins, but it was impossible, as we were only to stay a few hours.

Leaving Adelaide we steamed directly for Cape Leewin, which is at the southern extremity of Western Australia, and the last bit of land we should see until we sighted Cape Guardafui on the extreme eastern point of Africa.

In rounding Cape Leewin we experienced very dirty weather, several bullocks dying from the exposure on deck to the cold, or killed by the force of the waves which are always very rough at this point.

Quite a funny incident occurred at this time; it happened during my "saloon watch" from 12 to 2 a. m. The port-holes had all been snugly secured for the night in the saloon, and the passengers had been warned previously on no account to open those in the state rooms; but an obstinate John Bull, who thought he knew more than the officer on duty, ventured to disobey this order, and retired leaving the port-holes partially open.

He was rudely awakened from his slumbers by an unruly rush of waters through the port, that completely drenched the cabin, poured into his berth and half-drowned the occupant. Sputtering wildly and nearly choked with the salt water, he leaped from his bunk and rushed out into the saloon gasping out that he was drowning and the ship sinking. Guessing the cause of his fright, I ran into his state-room and waiting for a favorable lurch of the vessel managed to close the port and secure it before the water had a chance to force back into the cabin; but I had a nice task before me in mopping up the water we had shipped. I had one satisfaction, however; the passenger's clothes scattered through the state-room were drenched through with salt water and completely spoiled; it taught him such a lesson that rather than undergo a like experience again, he kept his port closed during the hottest nights while in the Red Sea and was almost suffocated.

After leaving Cape Leewin the weather moderated materially, but on our first Sunday at sea it was still too rough to hold services on deck, so they occurred in the main saloon, crew and passengers all being invited, the captain officiating. As I was very tired, I passed the hour in my "pew" taking a short rest and in appropriate meditation, subjected to a running fire of commentaries from my comrades who had also taken advantage of the temporary lull and were discussing current events, which were dished up in the choicest of cockney dialect.

We had about a dozen children among the saloon passengers, and two or three nurses. These were assigned to the children's table, and, greatly to my disgust, I was appointed purveyor. This meant so much extra work all through the voyage, as their meals occurring about half an hour before the regular meal time, I was expected to get everything cleared away before the next table was set, and then assist in getting the latter ready. There was certainly no idling on board the Chimborazo, and especially among the dwellers of the "Glory Hole."

I will give a brief *resume* of the day's labor, which will show more clearly how my time was occupied, and also how the long, monotonous days were passed, and this sketch represents not one, but every day of the long six weeks' voyage.

At a quarter to five the "deck man" stumbled down the companion into our den and aroused the tired occupants of the "pews" with a "Now then, tumble out, sleepy, two bells just struck, get up on deck!" and with many a yawn and half-muttered imprecation we lazily dress and seek the purer air above. Each man is supplied with a bucket and scrubbing brush at the beginning of the voyage, which he is expected to be responsible for, but the boys used to steal each other's brushes and erase the private marks, so that every morning would see some one minus either a bucket or brush engaged in a search after the missing article.

My first duty after tumbling out was to take my bucket and brush from where they were stowed away and scrub fifty feet of the main deck, which generally occupied an hour and half; a somewhat hard "eye-opener" to start in with. Then work for an hour in the saloon, polishing up the glasses in the racks, or the brass-work on the punkah rods. At 7:30 I went below to dress for the children's breakfast at eight. At nine occurred the regular saloon breakfast, after which we were permitted to eat our own meal, then more cleaning in the saloon, getting ready for inspection at eleven; polishing sky-lights or silverware took until twelve, when children's dinner had to be served up. Saloon lunch at one, after which, if it was no a "field day" (*i. e.* extra work, hauling stores or "humping spuds" from the store room forward, or passing up beer cases from the lazerette), we were allowed an hour or so of much needed rest. At five, children's tea, which I had to get ready alone; saloon dinner at six; our own at 7.30 p. m., which was followed immediately by saloon tea at eight.

Every other night my rest was broken by a midnight watch from 12 to 2, or 2 to 4, so that one can readily see that life on the Chimborazo was not a bed of down, by any means.

Our second Sunday at sea was marked by a burial, the first I had ever witnessed on the ocean. The day previous a young woman belonging in the steerage died of consumption. Her only relative on board was a brother, who was taking her back to Wales to die, knowing she was beyond recovery. He sobbed incessantly during the funeral service, and when the body, sewn up in canvas and weighted down with iron slugs, was shot over the side, he was with difficulty restrained from jumping over after it. Altogether it was a very affecting scene.

On the Wednesday following another death occurred, this time one of the saloon passengers. It happened during my watch. I had just returned from the "grand rounds" in the second cabin, and was trimming the oil lamp that swung from the rack, when I heard a faint cry issue from one of the state rooms. Knowing the doctor had been attending a sick passenger, I surmised at once from whence the sound issued and went hastily in. The poor fellow was gasping for breath and black in the face from his exertions. I rushed at once for the doctor, who came immediately, but before he reached the sick man's cabin, his services were not needed. The deceased was an invalid who had amassed a fortune in tin-mining in New South Wales, but had ruined his health in the struggle and died without reaping any benefit from his life-long exertions. He was buried next morning just before breakfast, at eight bells.

The passengers, as is usual, used to get up pools on the ship's run, and this excitement never flagged; in fact it was the one redeeming feature of the day, and as soon as the run was posted and the lucky fellow duly admired the passengers relapsed into their ordinary apathy and tried to kill time by reading flirting, card-playing or smoking, as their tastes or ambitions prompted. In a smaller way, we, of the rank and file, also made up pools among ourselves on the run, and one day after putting in a shilling and taking the only number left, I won the sweepstakes of fifteen shillings; the run was 297 miles. The next day the run was 312 miles, and my number was 313; it was close enough to be exasperating, but as I won several pools on the voyage, I came out ahead finally.

The third day of July was our third Sunday at sea, and as we were close to the Equator, the weather was very warm; but a good breeze was blowing which was very refreshing, and as we stood bare-headed listening to the captain as he read the service from the prayer-book, the sailors standing in a row with their bright blue jerseys, I thought I had never witnessed such a picturesque scene. The sea was like glass, the quarter deck almost clean enough to eat from, and the canvas flapping lazily overhead, seemed to swell the chorus of voices like that of an organ after the singing has subsided.

We celebrated the "glorious fourth" by crossing the Equator. The nearest approach to an American among the passengers was a Canadian, who however did the honors by getting up an entertainment in the smoking-room, assisted by three or four Englishmen. It was a nigger-minstrel show, professedly, but after the visitors had retired, brandy and soda, hock and champagne made an appearance, and the rest of the evening was devoted to convivialities of a very noisy nature. We also celebrated down in the "Glory Hole," I presiding. Lemonade and bottled beer were smuggled down early, and I invited the boys to drink to the health of the stars and stripes, which they heartily responded to with three cheers for "Yank."

The next morning we sighted Cape Guardafui, the first land we had seen in twenty days, after traversing nearly six thousand miles. The coast-line here is very bold and rugged, abounding with dangerous rocks, to which we gave a wide berth. The natives are said to be very savage and carnivorously disposed, hence our anxiety to keep a respectful distance. To-day I picked up a letter written by one of the children, who is on her way to England to visit her grandparents; it is written to her mother in Australia. As she could not mail it I kept it, out of curiosity; it is unique in its way, so I will copy it here:

"Near the Red Sea, July 5, 1881.
"My Dear Mamma:

"We have such funny cabins to sleep in, you have to hold on or else you fall out. They have a signal-light on board, so if anybody fell over, they could see the life buoy. We had a dance last night, it was very nice; we had a polka, a shotece (schottische) and a walse. It was too roly to walse, so we left off, then sang 'God save the Queen.' We went to bed after that.

SEVENTEENTH EXTRACT.

July 10th. To-day we sighted Aden, the coaling port of the Arabian shore for the Peninsular and Orient boats, but as we coal at Port Said, do not stop here.

July 11th. To-day we entered the Red Sea through Bab-el-Mandeb or "Gates of Hell." It is fearfully hot and this afternoon I took a salt-water bath in the bath-room. I found the water very buoyant but extremely salty.

"July 12th. This morning passed wreck of the "Duke of Lancaster," beached on the coast of Africa, and a little further on that of the "Penguin," standing upright high and dry in the sand; it is a sad and impressive sight to see these deserted vessels, away off on this inhospitable coast. We are drawing very near to Suez and expect to enter the canal in a day or two.

July 15th. To-day we entered the Great Canal; the entrance is close to the Government building which is composed of stone. We proceed very slowly, only five miles an hour. At night we made fast to the second station, vessels not being allowed to go on after dark. In company with some of the boys, I went in swimming after eight bells and swam over to Arabian and African shores, where I landed and took a run along the sandy beach. The current is very strong in the canal, running fully six miles an hour.

We arrived at Port Said early Sunday morning and were greeted by a big crowd of natives who flocked around the vessel offering their wares. We also took on 560 tons of coal inside three hours; this place and Singapore are considered the two fastest coaling stations in the world. We left Port Said in the afternoon and entered the Mediteranean Sea, which I gazed upon for the first time. Towards evening we passed very close to Alexandria and saw the lights of the port.

July 19th. Passed the Island of Crete at six o'clock this morning, noted as the place where Saint

Paul is said to have been wrecked on his voyage to Rome. Towards dark passed Mount Ætna, and at 10.30 p. m. entered the Straits of Messina. The night was beautifully clear and warm; did not retire until we had passed Stromboli at 1 a. m.

JULY 21st. Naples at last: The bay is very fine but somehow I cannot enthuse over it quite as much as did Byron. The view from Mount Vesuvius must be magnificent; regretted my inability to indulge in the experiment. Toward night the blue devils danced gayly as they issued from the mouth of the crater; the effect from our position in the bay being wierdly picturesque.

JULY 22d. Left Naples this morning, do not stop again until we reach Plymouth, our next port of call. Passed the Island of Sardinia, but too early to see anything and in fact too far off for any practical use.

JULY 25th. Early this morning passed Cape de Gata and at five o'clock sighted Gibraltar. I gazed on the huge mass of rock with peculiar feelings as I reflected on its past history. The main rock rises abruptly out of the sea and has two peaks, on the highest of which I could plainly see a signal station. The sides slope down and appeared to be thickly settled with dwelling-houses.

JULY 26th. Passed Cape de St. Vincent at ten this morning, and at seven in the evening passed Lisbon; could see nothing but a few scattered lights however. Water getting more choppy as we approach the Bay of Biscay. Passed Cape Finisterre at 8:30 p. m. and entered the Bay of Biscay at midnight.

We had a quick trip across to Plymouth and nothing of interest occurred beyond the death of a man in the steerage, who was buried just abreast of the Island of Ushant. Passed the new Eddystone Lighthouse just before dark and dropped anchor at eight o'clock in the bay at Plymouth. We had a pleasant trip up the English Channel, passengers all disembarking at Gravesend, after scattering largesse among the stewards. This latter was an English habit I was quickly initiated into and found it a most commendable practice so long as I was the recipient; I found it quite a bore later on.

At the Royal Albert Dock in London I said

farewell to my messmates and in the afternoon received my certificate of discharge and account of wages, which were given me at the Mercantile Marine Office at the Victoria Docks. Some day I intend having both documents framed and hang them in a cabinet along with several other souvenirs.

Prior to leaving Australia, I had written home. via San Francisco, to send all mail in care of the American Exchange; so that my first visit was directed there in the Strand, where I registered and was fortunate enough to receive several Chicago letters.

Next day I met two or three Chicago gentlemen at the Exchange, among others the well-known correspondent of a leading Chicago paper, who with his son gave me a cordial invitation to call at their headquarters close by. I also met several Board of Trade men whom I knew in Chicago, one a very near friend to whom I had said good-bye in San Francisco a year previous. He, with his wife, was then starting on a tour of the world, and left for Japan the week prior to my starting for Sandwich Islands. The meeting was a very pleasant one and over a charming little dinner at the Buckingham Palace Hotel, we exchanged a few notes on our year's travels.

Next day I took a trip down to Brighton on the coast and had a nice surf bath, which set me to reviewing the different waters I had bathed in: Atlantic, Pacific and Indian oceans; Australian and New Zealand waters; Red Sea and Suez Canal, and the great Salt Lake at Utah I counted as among the waters I had laved in, which I considered a goodly showing for a comparatively young traveler. Nile water I have drunk and like very much, but to bathe in the waters of the Congo river is ever my pet ambition.

Of course I visited Westminster Abbey, the Tower of London, British Museum and National Art Gallery while in London; for although I was in haste to get back to Chicago, the reputation of these places is world-wide, and I had long anticipated paying them a visit.

I celebrated my twenty-first birth-day by participating in a pic-nic excursion to old Epping Forest in the county of Essex, situated in the suburbs of East London and renowned as the country residence of Bluff King Hal. Everything was chatmingly English, and the quaint old driver with his rosy-tipped nose, who drove us there, was the living prototype of Dickens' "Tony Veller." Indeed I fairly revelled in Dickens' characters all the while I was in London.

The three weeks I spent in London and its suburbs were full of interest to me and I should like to have extended my visit, but the Atlantic was still to be crossed, and I had to take my chances at Liverpool for a ship, but of this I had little fear, as one of my passengers from Sydney, who had taken a sea-voyage for his health, was the manager of a line of steamers running between Liverpool and Montreal and had promised to help me to a berth.

I arrived at Liverpool at eight in the evening and early next morning repaired to the office of the company, managed by my "Chimborazo" acquaintance. By a great stroke of fortune, one of his ships was to leave that very day, having been delayed by bad weather for nearly ten hours. I was given a note to her captain; at ten o'clock had signed papers, and at noon we were steaming down the Mersey, en route for Quebec and Montreal.

I had a very easy time on the "Winnipeg," but it was simply because of the contrast between that and my billet on the "Chimborazo," as I was still very busy and found my time well occupied. We only had about thirty saloon passengers and carried but a few in the steerage.

The first week out we met with strong head winds and experienced pretty rough and rolling weather, but on the second Sunday we struck a perfect day, and all the passengers were on deck enjoying the beautiful weather. The sun shone grandly, while the old ocean was as calm and peaceful as an artificial lake, not a white-cap being visible to the eye.

We passed through a very thick fog as we entered the straits of Labrador and were obliged to run at half-speed until it lifted. Fortunately this was all the hazy weather we met with, so that our voyage was not delayed much by the vexatious fogs which are so prevalent in these regions.

On Monday early we entered St. Lawrence river, nine days from Liverpool, and at Father Point took on our pilot, anchoring at Point Levi, Quebec, just before midnight. Next day was spent in discharging part of the cargo, but we finally left for Montreal early Wednesday morning, arriving at the latter place on the day following.

From Montreal I went to New York and from thence to Chicago, arriving home after an absence of sixteen months, having about half the capital I started with; a record of about forty thousand miles of travel, which my readers can judge for themselves, whether or not, was full of adventure—and above all throughly convinced that America is the country of all countries to live in and Chicago the champion city of the world.

www.ingramcontent.com/pod-product-compliance
Lightning Source LLC
Chambersburg PA
CBHW020846160426
43192CB00007B/808